HOW TO STOP OVERTHINKING

ESCAPE ANXIETY AND OVERWHELM BY QUITTING GOAL SETTING'

LUKE JOHN HARRISON

Foreword by Brian Grasso

Let's Tell Your Story Publishing
London

COPYRIGHT

This book is dedicated to every person who struggles with their own self-doubt. This is for you.

Contents

ACKNOWLEDGEMENTS

I really would like to thank ...

Mam and Dad - for all your love and support through the years and for allowing me to follow my dreams.

Warwick, my best friend, my brother - for all that you are and the rock you've been in my life. This book would not have been possible without you.

Shaun Thompson, my other best friend, for the years of continued friendship and absolute trust. You are one of the most important men in my life.

Nick Tennant, another best friend of mine, although we don't see each other too often, you are one of my favourite people, my friend.

Paul Mort - You showed me another way, by just being your amazing self. I owe the start of loving myself to you.

Chris Brown - you got me the start in the industry of being an entrepreneur and I'm eternally grateful for your teachings.

Brian Grasso - you taught me to eliminate the limits I had placed on myself. Your belief in me has helped so wonderfully and, because of that, I'm able to share my true self with many others to this day.

Martin Rooney, Phil Richards, Dax Moy - You guys and your courses have blown my mind and added to my tools and philosophies, I can't thank you enough.

Tracey Holmes - One of the kindest, most wonderful hearted ladies I know. You've been a complete angel in my life since I met you. You are appreciated every single day.

Wayne Savage - the cover artist and man who did all the wonderful art for the book, you're a star buddy. Check out www.facebook.com/crazycartoonsandcaricatures

The initial test readers, Ruth Goodwin, Paul Bubbin McNulty, Lee McFarlane, Darren Barrett, Michelle Douglas.

My family, who are always a great inspiration, Lisa Murray and Neil Murray, James Holloway, my late Grandma Mable and all my other close family, you know who you are.

All past and current members of the Total Fitness Tribe, You guys are always a reason for me to keep going, you always inspire

Every past and current #calmmotherfuckers mentorship client. You guys have no idea what an honour it is to serve you all.

The crew and cast of BBC 2's 'Special Forces: Ultimate Hell week - for giving me an experience I'll cherish forever.

Colette Mason - For helping me with getting this book done and out to the masses, you're one of a kind.

My Tuesday night gaming group - Tim, James, Neil, Shaun and Warwick - You make every Tuesday spectacular.

Steve Bagnal - For being an awesome coach and a great consistent training partner all these years #Ibelieveinsteve

All my followers, watchers and friends from Facebook and all social media platforms which have supported me over the years.

FOREWORD

"Until you make the unconscious conscious, it will direct your life and you will call it fate."

That quote from Carl Jung is a game-changer.

And a life-changer, if you just pause to give it some reflection.

Whether you know me personally or 'know' me through Facebook, you wouldn't have recognised the person I was had we been friends 10 years ago.

I was angry, frustrated, jealous, jaded, but mostly, so terribly sad.

Sad because I had tried absolutely everything you were supposed to try. I followed the goal setting experts, listened to the success gurus, and did the work that the 'hustle' authorities claim is required.

None of it worked for me.

My days were spent in this frenzy of commotion. Charting my goals, reading every book I could get my hands on and working my ass off to make it all come together.

In contrast, my nights were spent in a pit of grief,

in disbelief that I would ever achieve my goals and absolutely exhausted from another 24-hour cycle of trying to make it happen.

I started believing that I was broken and that, while my friends and colleagues were crushing it and on the cusp of even greater heights, I was bound for mediocrity, destined to be inferior.

I thought that, somehow, I lacked the smarts, the ability or the savvy to achieve what I wanted. That was my fate.

Until I started making my unconscious conscious.

The game-changer and life-changer for me had nothing to do with setting more goals, reading more books or hustling harder. It had to do with learning to understand what mindset is, how it works and how mine was keeping me stuck.

Success - so I came to realise - wasn't about working to become successful, so much as releasing yourself from the reasons you're not.

And the reason I wasn't?

I overthought EVERYTHING. Absolutely everything. From decisions in business to decision in diet. From considerations in dating to considerations in fitness.

Overthinking was the cause and source of something both you and I know very well - self-sabotage.

I knew what to do and, in most cases, even how to do it, but there was something preventing me from actually getting it done.

If you've wanted to make more money, grow a successful business or finally make real the dream you've been carrying in your heart - but can't - no matter what you do or how hard you try, then I'd ask you to give this book, by my dear friend Luke John Harrison, a very serious read.

He is the real deal.

And his content will change your life.

Sincerely,

Brian J Grasso

INTRODUCTION

ABOUT ME

Hi, Luke here. This is my first book as a mindset coach. I struggled with overthinking for many years, but now I've helped hundreds of people overcome anxiety and overthinking through personal online one-to-one mindset mentorships.

I run the North-East's premier fitness training facility, Total Fitness Tribe'.

I've mentored with some of the world's best in mindset and lifestyle creation, notably Tony Robbins, Brian Grasso, Dax

Moy, Phil Richards, Jordan Belfort, Martin Rooney, Paul Mort and many more.

I inspire and impact people day in and day out via my #dailyboom social media series.

I'm a public speaker at workplaces, training events and courses.

I'm the guy people can lean on and trust to understand them without judgement.

I'm a qualified personal trainer, problem solver and, in my previous life, plumber as well.

I believe you need to be an overachiever in helping people push through their barriers and limiting beliefs so that they live a life free from their trapped thoughts.

HOW OVERTHINKING TOOK OVER MY LIFE

I had a good upbringing with two parents that loved and cared for me, Mam a charity worker, Dad a fire fighter. We were never in any way rich, my parents did what they could and I feel very grateful for what they did for me. I feel I came from humble beginnings and was never given everything I wanted, but got everything I needed.

But, around four years ago in 2012, this was when it all began to change for me.

I had been a fulltime plumber for eight years and was hitting a low point in my life. I'd had a string of several failed relationships, several years of weekend drug and alcohol usage, a lot of womanising, nearly got sacked from my work and at one point, when the shit was really hitting the fan from all sides, I briefly considered taking my own life.

When I was a plumber, I had job security, holiday pay, sick pay, a good pension and a fixed routine, I had a mortgage, an Audi car and a pretty tidy wage for someone in their 20s.

But I was miserable, unfulfilled, pissed off and ratty.

And every Sunday night I'd get that feeling in my stomach, the knots of overwhelm, anxiety and fear that I wouldn't be able to handle it. I can't remember when it started exactly, but it went this way for several months. I just didn't want to wake up to the day and face it all.

Yet I would put on my 'happy mask' because 'nowt's a bother' right?

Man. I was full of shit.

Maybe you've felt lost like that too?

I needed to be honest that I wasn't happy. I was LYING to myself and everyone else. Seriously. I kept lying to myself that it was cool and I should feel 'lucky' to have a secure job and a house and others that cared for me. And I felt compelled to agree. I hid the truth for fear of judgement. I was a MAN and we're supposed to 'keep it together' right?

Then, one day, it hit me.

I thought to myself, "can I live the next 40+ years of my life truly happy like this?"

FUCK!

Like being slapped in the face with a wet salmon, I realised the power in the honest answer to this. And I say honest because, in the past, I was always quick to justify an answer like 'Yeah, it's ok', when I was lying through my teeth.

And here's the first thing with 'truly happy'. Most people have no idea what that even means.

I didn't.

So, the first thing that came to mind when I answered that question (after the initial crippling fear of trying anything BUT what I knew) was

HOW?

- ✿ how do I get out
- ✿ how do I leave
- ✿ how do I become happier
- ✿ how. .how... how....

Then I'd get overwhelmed, scared and do nothing.

Sound familiar?

So, months passed where I kept asking 'how', looking online at successful people and thinking, 'how did they do it?'

Which led to guess what? More overwhelm. More overthinking.

Which turned into procrastination, then fear of it not working out.

And, so, it was back to acting comfortable.

But guess what.

Comfortable for me was *MISERABLE.*

WHY I WROTE THIS BOOK

The answer is very simple. I used to be very sad and unfulfilled and I found goal setting didn't work too well for me.

I've set so many goals in my life, yet achieved a lot fewer of them.

I felt stupid when I didn't do what I said I would. I found that these 'goals' sounded great, but they had very little focus apart from

☀ 'I want to make £x in x days'

or

☀ 'I want to be able to look like x in x months'

They were never profound enough to get massively excited about, and, as soon as something new and more exciting came along, I'd look to that, get distracted and fail. Again. These re-peated failures were always a blow to my self-esteem and confidence. I felt worthless and insignificant.

One of the most important things to human nature is the need to feel significant. That's why you set goals, isn't it? So you can feel your life has purpose. So you can feel proud and peo-ple will say things like 'good on you' or 'well done.' It gives meaning to what you do and makes you feel significant.

You may say you don't do it for the recognition, but you want to feel significant right? Special? Needed? Wanted?

When you're struggling, it's hard to tell anyone how bad things have got. It's tempting to take the easy route and keep living the lie.

It's time to stop forcing yourself to 'man up' and come up with a new way of living.

Us men have egos. Egos can actually be powerful, positive things when used correctly. But, when they're knocked, es-pecially when you're struggling, the last thing you want to say is that it's all getting a bit much.

You don't want to seem weak or like you can't handle it, be-cause you're an adult and you're supposed to cope with this stuff.

Absolute bullshit.

This is why there's so many people who slide into depression.

When do you step back and say

"Hey, I'm mega-struggling here... It's hard... I'm con-
fused... I feel I've lost myself... I can't see a way to get
back to feeling happy."

When you're feeling down, it's easy to get preoccupied with
what's going wrong. I felt it myself, and I've seen it many
times with the people who I've helped.

It's easy to dwell on

- the problems you face
- the people who let you down
- the situations you're struggling with
- the environment you're stuck in
- the work colleagues who don't care
- the lack of excitement

and on and on and on.

Ninety-nine per cent of the problems in people's heads stem
from the thought of a perceived lack of something. Such as

I don't have x, so I'm unhappy.

Have you ever felt the underlying reason for your unhappi-
ness is because you don't have what you think will make you
happy? Even though you have no idea if it will make you
happy, because you haven't got it?

Because you're always striving to put things right, you end
up feeling overwhelmed. Man, I hate overwhelm. It's crippling, isn't it?

ıy thoughts, so little time
ıy tasks, so little energy
y problems, not enough solutions

ıⱺⱺe s little quote for you from Brian Grasso,

"Happiness is not about finding reasons to make us happy. It's about releasing us from the reasons we're not happy."

WHO THIS BOOK IS FOR

It's for people like me! People who struggle with overthinking, worrying, procrastinating, lack of self-worth.

It's for people who have failed lots of goal setting attempts.

Maybe you're sick of your job or current business and want to change, but you're terrified.

Perhaps confidence is an issue in certain areas and you're struggling to understand your thoughts and emotions.

So, if you

- ✿ are a business owner or career-minded
- ✿ want a more fulfilling life
- ✿ struggle with over thinking
- ✿ feel insular and lonely
- ✿ lurch from one quick fix to the next

and, very importantly,

✧ have tried goal setting and found it didn't work for you

then THIS BOOK is for you! :-).

HOW TO USE THIS BOOK

I recommend you read this book from start to finish, rather than dipping in and out of sections that catch your eye.

Use a highlighter pen to mark any areas which stand out for you. Active learning helps things to stick in your mind.

I've deliberately kept this book simple. The brain likes to focus on just one thing at a time.

I have included lots of anecdotes from my life, not because I love to talk about myself, but because I have put in some hard yards and learned many a difficult lesson.

I have shared these stories with you to spare you some pain, delay or hardship in your progress. You'll also definitely not think "Why does this crap only happen to me!!!" I've had plenty of calamities too, trust me.

Use the progress sheets.

I've put two styles of progress sheets together to help motivate you, help you track how you're doing and keep you focused. There is a weekly and a daily progress tracking sheet.

You can download and print out your own copies at www.howtostopoverthinking.com.

I will teach you how to use these sheets to set weekly intentions, designed to forge your personal progress rather than set specific 'goals'.

You will need to complete your

- ☼ weekly 4 Ps intentions sheet
- ☼ daily progress sheets

to get the most out of following my system.

Using these sheets, you will understand that *PROGRESS is more important than GOAL SETTING.* I'm here to get your mind and behaviour shifted to focusing on positive progress in your life. And *NOTHING* else.

YOU ARE NOT ALONE

Fear, worries, frustrations, impatience, anger, can happen to all of us.

I'm actually writing this and I'm apprehensive about what I'm going to say or how I'm going to say it. I mean, holy shit, at 30 years old, I'm actually writing my very first book.

A former drug-taking, womanising plumber from a little poverty town in the UK, sat in a first class train carriage furiously planning my own book while overthinking, procrastinating and worrying about future judgement.

I'm actually worried.

What are 'they' are going to think of me? What are you going to think of this book! Will I do myself proud? Will I make a tit out of myself?

You could say there's the first lesson in this journey.

If I can write a book in a state of fear, don't you think you can push forward a little bit in your life?

Of course you can.

And I'm going to share with you exactly how in the coming pages.

The book will to take you on a journey, through my system for getting the life you want, by sharing thoughts, personal struggles and experiences that have helped shape me into the ever growing man I am today. Notice how I didn't say 'strong', 'motivated'...

The focus, of this entire book (and my life right now) is on growing and expanding via progress.

I'll never be perfect, neither will you be. I am humbled to say it, but perfection doesn't exist.

Even if your Instagram or Facebook shows it :-).

I'm a normal person, just like you, who was born with the same capabilities, limits and potential.

But then what happens is 'life' forms us.

An accumulation of influences form your perceptions of what should be, which leads you to your ever comfortable belief systems that you carry, which, in turn, form your expectations.

And guess what, whatever you expect to happen, usually does!

How many times have you expected something to go wrong and it goes completely tits up?

You know what I'm talking about, right?

Let me show you this sequence in simpler terms...

INFLUENCE >> PERCEPTION >> BELIEF >> EXPECTATIONS
(WHAT ACTUALLY
HAPPENS)

I like to think that, throughout life, you grow and adapt, but mostly, you know what, you really do.

You learn how to conform, act, behave and *think*.

School, parents, friends, social media, environment, society, etc., are the *influences* that form our entire being.

And guess what they place upon us?

Limitations.

Have you ever noticed how things seem laid out for you in life? There is that compulsion to follow certain paths, gain certain grades, give in to the peer pressure of the school and work system.

If you can 'choose' your path, your 'lifestyle,' why are so many of us hitting a point where, like a bolt out of the blue, we think 'how the fuck did I end up here?!'

Do you remember this question from when you were younger...

So, what do you want to be when you grow up?

To which you'd reply something like 'a doctor', 'accountant' or 'a teacher' or 'an astronaut.'

...or, if you're like me, you might say something like 'male stripper.' (No shit.)

Have you noticed, you tend to answer using a profession. What if you were asked a different question?

Who do you want to BECOME when you grow up?

How much more impactful would that be?

Social status, peer pressure, societal, cultural and environmental influences shape how you should think, act and be. These factors tend to dictate 'how it should be.'

Well, I'm here to call bullshit.

In 2013, when I quit my job as a fulltime plumber for a local construction firm to go it alone with my own business, the trigger was asking myself that very question.

Who do I want to become?

(When I eventually grow up, ha, ha!)

Not...

"What do I want to be"

WHO DO YOU WANT TO BECOME

So, let's start there my friend, *WHO* are you?

Really, who are you - not what do you 'do' for a living but who are you deep down?

As an adult, have you been told you're supposed to 'keep it together', right?

Well, that's all bullshit. Sometimes you need to be honest with someone and actually admit you need some support, guidance and accountability to 'get back on track'.

For me, that moment of needing to reach out came when I was crippled with overthinking as I tried to leave my plumbing job.

FROM ANXIOUS PLUMBER TO MINDSET COACH

When I wanted to quit plumbing, I felt scared and alone. I was the only one of my circle of friends and family who decided to take the big leap. Everyone else was still stuck in their little ruts.

Months of procrastinating and worrying came before I actually left my job. I fitted in my gym instructor course on a weekend, while I was still in my fulltime job.

It took about six months or so before I was 'qualified', and, throughout that time, I still had to keep battling on with my miserable plumbing job.

I asked myself the question "How much longer am I prepared to stay miserable for?"

A weekend event I attended in Manchester made me make the decision to leave my job by the following April. That gave me six months.

Sometimes, it takes just one person to make you believe in yourself. That one person (at that event) was Paul Mort. A man who I'll always admire. He gave me the belief in me before I had it in myself. I created a self-made deadline to get my ass into gear.

"Time to get my shit together", I thought. It was hugely satisfying to know I was on my way out my job, but here's the truth. I was still terrified. Waking up in anxious fear. I even took two weeks off work on the sick with 'stress'.

I went to the doctors, explained my symptoms and he prescribed me 'beta blockers' as he told me "You've got anxiety," I had no fucking clue what that was.

As a bloke who weight trained and was a bit of a hit with the ladies. I was thinking that my ego was hit. "I'm a man! I don't have time to be feeling like this!" Reality was, once again, that I was full of shit!

I wasn't ok and 'optimistic'. I was struggling and over-whelmed. I wasn't excited and 'pumped'! I was in pain and absolutely terrified! But I was embarrassed to admit any of this.

At work, I had to face a disciplinary for some 'crap work I'd done. I tried to defend myself, but got a final written warning and was nearly sacked. It hurt my ego. Truth was, I just didn't care, the people, the system. I hated it all. Deep down, I actually hated the person I was becoming - that short-tempered, angry, anxious bastard I saw looking back at me in the mirror.

From the written warning, I still had to make it to April and save up money to actually live while working on a new life-style.

I had no idea HOW I was going to do it.

The logistics, the whole 'ins and out's' were very uncertain. But, after meeting a mate for coffee and seeking out a mentor, calling everyone in my phonebook, I decided to ask people to come join my outdoor 'bootcamp'.

Then it began. I took nine people to a car park by a local beach. I bought a small music system and my first session was 6:15am Monday morning, January 2013, and it was freezing!

After that session I got in my car, did my eight-hour shift plumbing, then came back to the beach at 6:15pm till 7pm to teach again, then answered Facebook messages and emails and researched online till about 11pm, then went to bed.

This hellish lifestyle continued for a few months until February, where I handed in my notice. I'll never forget the relief.

I still had a mortgage that I couldn't afford to sustain so I moved out of my house and back with my parents and grew my project, The Total Fitness Tribe in South Shields, which has become the most expensive training facility in the North-East - not bad for someone who didn't even know where to begin!

None of it came without sacrifice though and I'll continue to share more of this journey. I actually lived (illegally) above my facility for a short while too, woke up with frost on my head, no wash facilities and lived off takeaways for about six months. Without struggle there really is no progress. I'll share later on how I made the front page news because I mentioned the word 'terrorist'... yup, strap yourself in my friend, there's so much more to come.

You're probably wondering, "that's all well and good Luke, you're sorted." You stopped being plumber, blah, blah...

"but how do I personally make the changes I need in my life?"

You may well ask?

The one big thing I'd like you to consider if why you haven't made that leap or changed your life, and how you'd like to right now, could boil down to one simple thing.

YOU SIMPLY HAVEN'T BEEN IN ENOUGH PAIN YET.

Ouch!

That idea may sting a little and make you frown upon reading those words.

But, consider any time in your life where you've hit the 'fuck it' switch and never gone back to something...

- ✷ that diet you tried
- ✷ that gym you joined
- ✷ that relationship you ended
- ✷ that friend you ditched because they crapped all over you...

You have drawn a line in the sand and *DECIDED* you've had enough of the intense pain / frustration, and you leave it behind - for good.

The good news is, you can use that *FUCK IT AND WALK AWAY* principle to make some positive changes in your life.

You *DECIDE* to take some *ACTION*, and work towards a new *GOAL*, do some 'things' and, usually, you make a little *PRO-GRESS.*

And that progress makes you feel good about yourself right?

But sometimes that changes.

Your progress shudders to a halt. It's like you have hit a brick wall, and you start to uncontrollably slip back into your old way of life. You start texting your ex, that friend who crapped over you is back on the scene.

Sound familiar?

So, how do you fix it?

People fail when this happens

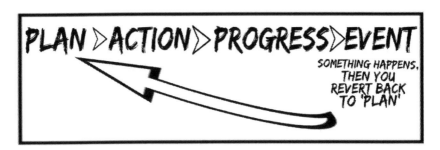

There's a missing piece to this flow and, believe it or not, it's the only piece that needs to be put into place for you to achieve what you set out to do.

This piece fits in before all the planning, action and progress.

It's the one thing you're missing...

It's a *DECISION.* (No shit!)

You can make all the goals, dreams, vision boards and share ALL the positive affirmations you want, but until you say to yourself "*ENOUGH IS ENOUGH* or "*FUCK THIS!* and make the decision to never go back to your old ways again you'll keep living the cycle of starting, stopping, starting, stopping...

HOW TO MAKE A DECISION

It's a simple process really, but, remember, simple does not always mean EASY.

You get in this life what you tolerate. How much longer can you tolerate your own bullshit? That's the biggest thing that's keeping you stuck where you are right now. The biggest bit of bullshit people create is thinking their 'excuses' for not doing something are genuine 'reasons'...

Take this example...

- ☼ "I haven't got time to prepare healthy food."
- ☼ "I just can't afford it."
- ☼ "I don't know enough yet."
- ☼ "It was my mate's, cousin's birthday, so I had to have a drink."

Are these really genuine reasons? Or is it just that you're too weak to say 'I'm not prepared to tolerate the bullshit anymore..'? To be pessimistic and doubtful of you changing things is gutless. To be optimistic and actually make a solid decision that you want more from your life and don't want to continue complaining about the way things are is damn courageous.

Let's look at the sequence you need to follow to really get results and stay on track.

DECISION ▷ PLAN ▷ ACTION ▷ PROGRESS

This is how we begin to impact our very lifestyle by adding the decision *FIRST* :-) Making a concrete decision is extremely powerful. You don't need anyone's permission, you only need your own. What decision is it you'd love to make that you've been holding back on?

Great examples I've helped other people realise are to

- quit accepting other people's opinions as gospel
- be able to say YES to exercise regularly
- give up alcohol during the week
- not allow yourself anything crap to eat UNTIL you've exercised
- no longer be prepared to put up with people's drama at home and work.
- never EVER diet again and adopt a healthy, balanced lifestyle, that includes regular exercise

All these are great examples that I've helped people adopt. Once they've made the decision, then we formulate a plan, get some action done and what we see are results, then we just continue and expect problems along the way. And what do we do when we face them? you may ask? We look for a solution...

What decision is it that you need to make?

DITCH GOAL SETTING FOR PROGRESS

Yep, you heard it right. Here's a book explaining about how to get the life you want - by ditching goal setting!

The decisions I want you to make are different to the decisions you make with traditional goal setting.

It took me a good few years to realise the goals I dreamed of, wrote down and tried to "hustle" towards were seldom achieved.

As your goal success eludes you, you get disheartened and pray for another distraction to keep you from feeling so bad. (For me, cue porn, too much social media or whatever else would divert my attention from feeling like a total loser).

Deep down, when I set 'goals' and didn't achieve them, I felt undeserving and questioned whether I was good enough.

Of course, I'd still follow and post positive affirmations on Facebook and be all *"Go for your goals guys! Don't let anyone bring you down!!"*

And, when I went to post this bullshit, I'd look at other folk on social media, seeing them *"KILLING IT"* or what not, and get envious and feel sad that I couldn't keep up.

I was spinning my wheels. I needed another way.

WHY GOAL SETTING DOESN'T WORK FOR YOU

Before you go any further, I don't want to get all arsey and slate 'goal setting', because it does have its place in life. There's no doubt that a lot of 'real-world results' rubbish my gloomy opinion on goal setting.

Yeah, there is lots of evidence to say goal setting does indeed work...

...but only for *SOME PEOPLE*...

SOME people, being the important thing to remember.

If you fall into the category of 'some people', then, like me, you need something else to keep you happy, that you can do at your own pace, that gets results so you don't end up feeling like a failure and falling off the wagon again.

NOT ACHIEVING GOALS HURTS

Ever felt like a failure? Have your friends ever said

> *Hey how's that thing you were gonna do going?'*

And you've failed. You have done fuck all about it.

Man, that sucks.

Why?

Well, there's a lot of pressure to uphold a certain image and be the 'rock' of many people. Plus you're trying to keep up with the "highlight reelers" on social media.

I remember feeling that pressure very well.

WHEN I LOOKED STUPID IN FRONT OF 15 ENTREPRENEURS

I once got up in the middle of a room on a course and stated out loud, bold as brass.

"I will DOUBLE MY INCOME in the next 90 days!"

And I didn't.

That made me feel like a total tit - a complete loser.

Why didn't it happen?

I'd set a 'goal' without thinking clearly about where I was or, indeed, how I was going to overcome obstacles.

I forgot that, when you strive to better yourself, you face problems. And when I didn't feel like pushing forward to get past those obstacles, I'd quit for a bit.

When I became stuck, I'd distract myself with porn or social media and I'd waste time. I wasn't committed enough to the cause. I carried things out based on feeling, but not making genuine commitment.

So, if I didn't *FEEL* like marketing that day, I'd just say *TO-MORROW.* Or, if I didn't feel like eating well or training that day, I'd just think *TODAY'S A REST DAY, I'LL GET BACK ON IT TOMORROW,* not realising I had very little commitment to the thing that I believed I wanted. No wonder I failed.

It's our daily rituals that define our success. You could call them 'habits', but a ritual is something you do that requires little to no willpower.

It's something you *MUST* do.

What does *MUST* mean? You'll do *'THAT THING'*

✿ regardless of how tired, angry, or sceptical you are
✿ regardless of the weather
✿ regardless of the day of the week or the month of the year
✿ regardless of whether someone has upset you or you've done something wrong

You do what you *MUST* do (your rituals). You need to hold yourself accountable.

After that course, I was left to my own devices to 'double my income'. Yes, I had all these great ideas and strategies, but no one on my case to make sure I acted on those new skills.

And that's why people mostly fail with goal setting, my friend. Because there's nothing and no one to hold us accountable.

And if you've failed before without accountability and a real plan of some sort, guess what? You'll fail again and again.

HOW TO GET THE LIFE YOU WANT WITHOUT GOAL SETTING

Here's my 'hack/secret/thing' or whatever the cool kids are naming it these days.

It's what I focus on to get what I want. It's the one ritual, that I believe is the most simple (but not easy) way to achieve what matters to you.

Want to know what it is?

Focus on progress.

Yep. That's it. Stop goal setting and ask yourself

- ✹ how can I progress from here
- ✹ what's the next step

You don't need a laser-focused '5-year plan' or a technicolour 'vision board' to succeed.

You need to focus on *GETTING BETTER*.

Have you noticed that lots of people are saying, "*I wish that things were better*", and, for some reason, nothing happens?

Have you ever heard them say, "*I wish that I was better.*"

I'm guessing no.

Why? Because progress all starts with you taking action, my friend. Nothing good ever happens by wishing and hoping things would magically change.

GET ONBOARD THE PROGRESS TRAIN

"The progress train?!" Maybe it sounds a bit cheesy, but, hey, it absolutely works!

This train is my metaphor for explaining how to make better decisions and, through those better decisions, improve your life.

Have you ever said "*I fell off track*" or maybe "*I fell off the wagon*"? I know I have - massively.

And here's why you always say those phrases.

Because tracks and wagons are designed to take things somewhere!

Funny that, right?

You, as a human need, to feel like you're going somewhere, and, if you're not, you feel like you fell off and you're stuck. Put your focus towards making progress and I guarantee you'll feel better in a very short amount of time. Remember,

Progress equals happiness.

PROGRESS IS AN ELASTIC 'GOAL'

Thing is with progress is that it can happen in seconds. You can make the instant decision to make progress

- ✿ invest in a course
- ✿ leave a job
- ✿ make a sale
- ✿ pick the phone up to have that awkward conversation
- ✿ leave a partner
- ✿ head out to the movies

Whatever decision you make, if it's guided with a focus on progress, you can *INSTANTLY* feel better.

Sometimes, it's not instant. Other progress that is life- changing can take weeks, months or years, like

- ✿ working out to get back in shape
- ✿ paying off your mortgage
- ✿ building a supportive network of like-minded people around you

All the stuff mentioned above is progress. It's just the rate that changes, i.e. how fast you'll achieve it once you have decided to make that change.

Certain people attain progress quicker than others. You're probably eager for change right away. *RIGHT NOW.* And that's understandable, particularly when you find yourself in a crappy situation.

But sometimes life is a marathon, not a sprint.

Progress comes from effort.

Sorry to break it to you, but there is no substitute for hard work. You just can't wave a magic wand and fix things over-night. You need to understand this simple rule, because patience is an important part of getting what you want out of life.

The effort that you see in front of you can be off-putting sometimes, I get it. Let me tell you how I discovered the power of progress.

WHEN I BECAME A GYM RAT

At our school, I was lucky enough to have a weights room in our sports hall. And, in that weights room, for the first time I could remember, I discovered something that I actually had a slight advantage in! I was a little bit stronger than most of the other kids in my class.

Bearing in mind my other sporting abilities were piss poor – I couldn't kick a ball, was hopelessly uncoordinated, and always the last to be picked for the team – I welcomed my discovery!

After all those years of sucking at everything 'sporty', I stumbled into something I really liked, and was good at!

This wasn't my 'golden ticket to glory'. I still sucked at the weights and had a way to go honing my skills. But, instantly, I found something that made me feel good, something I felt I could get real benefit from in my life.

I got instant progress when I started, and I automatically stuck with it because I saw progress.

There's a great lesson right there in that.

If you're good at something and it makes you feel good, go with it!

But not only that, the power of starting something is profound. Sometimes you procrastinate so much that, if you just started you'd see progress and be so much more enthusiastic to continue.

Since that moment in the weights room (now 16 years later) I'm still lifting weights. It became a habit - part of my daily rituals. My weightlifting ritual has made me into a more confident, stronger person. This, in turn, has helped me keep motivated and challenged, so that I progress in other areas of my life, like business and relationship building, too.

It also taught me that, sometimes, when focusing on progress, your 'goals' become elastic.

When I was lifting weights, I always saw progress, because that concrete end goal was never there. Once I could do a certain number of bench presses at a certain weight, there were always more repetitions to complete a set, or bigger weights to shift.

There was no end point set in stone. There was no specific goal to reach, attain and then give up on. I showed up, and kept going, because all I wanted was to be fitter and stronger.

A lot of people who set 'goals' (I believe) place a limitation on themselves. As, once you've achieved it, you usually stop and go back to your old way of doing things. For example, how many times have you lost some weight, then seen it yo-yo back on again?

If the 'goal' is elastic (like progress), you can *keep going* more easily.

Since then, I've discovered this progress philosophy of mine can work for many areas of life, not just pumping iron down the gym.

And that, my friend, is incredibly powerful!

PROGRESS IS GRADUAL BUT IT WORKS

It's important to remember these changes are often not instant. It's the cumulative effect of doing something consistently that brings the magic.

Wanna know the simple formula for success?

SIMPLICITY ✚ CONSISTENCY ▬ SUCCESS

Several times when I was lifting weights, there would be setbacks. I'd get injured, sometimes to the point where I could barely walk. I've strained my shoulder, tweaked my knee, been in so much pain I couldn't lift my arms or laugh because I was so sore.

I still kept showing up.

Becoming stronger didn't happen the first time I lifted the weights back at school. It took years to master certain lifts.

I'm still learning now.

But the beauty about using elastic progress as your motivation and not a 'finite goal' is that there are endless possibilities.

You can always challenge yourself to progress further and further.

What's more, the mental boost you get when you achieve something good in one area of your life, spurs you on to progress in other areas too.

SAYING FAREWELL TO PIZZA AND CHIPS

My efforts in the gym were going well, but I knew I needed to change what I was eating too. This is the bit *EVERYONE* struggles with.

Changing my diet was *HARD*. Going from pizza, chips and bread every week to steak, vegetables and nuts wasn't an easy change, but, gradually, I knew I needed better choices if I wanted to become stronger.

I needed to make progress with my nutrition, not just my fitness levels. The progress I was making with the gym put the fire in my belly to begin to eat right.

PATIENCE AND PROGRESS

It's the one word you constantly say you have not very much of, right... patience...

But, trust me, if you want to succeed in any area of your life, you must work on it.

Because the ones that lack patience are the ones who continually fail. You must understand life is mostly gradual when it comes to progress. The formula I shared before, simplicity + consistency = success, is entirely true.

To put it another way, to succeed you *MUST* be patient, because it takes consistency to succeed.

Most people can't be consistent because they're impatient. Let me be clear - there is no magic pill or potion, fairy godmother or a genie in a bottle that will get you instant results.

If you want results now, today, then you're reading the wrong book. Life results take work and the patience of continually *doing the work*.

Thankfully, patience (like most things) *can* be improved. It too can progress. How?

Because *YOU CAN PROGRESS.*

Because *YOU CAN IMPROVE.*

And how do you improve, exactly?

You get aboard the progress train, that cheesy thing I mentioned at the start of the chapter.

Let me tell you how this works. I'm excited...

Take a moment to look at the diagram on the previous page.

It illustrates what happens in life when you focus on PRO-GRESS, i.e. moving forward, step-by-step, rather than charging off to hit a goal, and coming off the rails when you overwhelm yourself and throw in the 'fuck it' card.

Think of the train, travelling up the tracks towards that thing on the horizon called *progress*, listed at the top.

In this representation, you are the "I'm worth it" train. Depending on where your focus is will ultimately decide where you will go. Because, where your focus goes, your energy flows. When your train is on the tracks, it must follow them. Yes, You can either go forwards towards progress, or, of course, backwards towards square one. There is no 'side-to-side' option.

The beauty of this explanation is that it demonstrates there are only two options for how your life is going to work - either getting further towards progress, growing and learning, or further away from progress, slowly getting worse.

Now, like trains in real life, they do have a destination, but once reached, they come back again and have another desti-nation, there really is no 'end' to a train's journey. It goes toward the destination, gets there, then progresses to it's next destination. It might turn around and go back again, but it's still moving forward and going somewhere.

Along the way, the train stops prior to that so called 'destina-tion'. It reaches somewhere. Then goes somewhere else. It reaches that place, then goes somewhere else, and so on. This should be your life my friend. No actual 'finish point', but a constant journey, progressing, moving forward and stopping from time to time along the way, making choices and then moving forward again -this is life. One big journey, the only end destination, as we know, is death. That's the only certainty in this life.

It's understandable you have a busy life and, with endless "to do lists" and distractions, you sometimes tend not to see the progress you make. It's easy to lose sight of where you are amongst the pressures of life. You're not constantly patting yourself on the back about a job well done, you're distracted by your responsibilities. The positive changes lose their prominence and, sometimes, you feel like you're stuck, when you're not. This is why I believe the train diagram is very powerful for your perspective and to remember your focus should always be on progress and your own personal set intentions.

Imagine when your train pulls into a station.

When you hit a station, you make a choice. You can stay on the train and do nothing and wait for a bit, or you can make a decision to get off the train and do something.

I've shown this idea on the diagram as a pair of choices - a 'good one' and a 'not so good one'.

Most people decide there's just one choice when their train comes to a stop. Needless to say, that tends to be the 'not so good option', because those options tend to need less will-power or effort.

But, have a look at the diagram again. You'll see there are at least two choices at a stop.

On the left-hand platform, you'll see good choices that will boost your progress. At the same stops there is a 'not so good' choice on the right-hand platform that will hinder your progress.

(Let's leave out 'bad' choices for now, I'll explain why shortly).

Imagine your progress train stops because something's happened – let's say you've had an argument with someone close to you.

You react negatively as you reckon they were in the wrong. The chances are, they think you're in the wrong too, and things escalate.

At this point, it's common to get out of each other's faces and have a few hours apart. You might go to the shop, buy some wine and a takeaway pizza and get pissed watching TV, whilst bitching about the other person to a friend on the phone.

The other person might head to the gym, work off the pent-up frustration, then call up a mate and ask for some advice on how to resolve the problem.

Who made the better choice?

Well, that's down to opinion, but you always do what you believe is best for you at the time. Just like the other person did. You were both at the same stop, with the same two choices, and yet two different decisions were made. Remember that.

You both *CHOSE* to do those things at the same stop. Both choices were available to both people. Both choices were under each person's control. Except you chose the "not so good" option.

GOOD CHOICES	NOT SO GOOD CHOICES
✿ work out to relieve stress ✿ keep in shape and boost confidence ✿ talk over options with a friend	✿ couch potato session ✿ drink alcohol numb stress ✿ binge on junk food ✿ whinge to a friend

The sooner you start realising it's you who needs to take responsibility for where you are and, ultimately, where you're going, the better.

The sooner you take responsibility for why you keep coming off the rails', the sooner your life begins to change.

It's not about blame, but responsibility. You're the driver, you've pulled into the stop. You can choose which platform you spend time at before getting going again.

The first step towards freedom from your not so good choices is knowing yourself and why you choose to go to those right-hand platforms.

TASK: WHERE DOES YOUR TRAIN STOP

Have another look at my progress train diagram. Can you spot the stops you're frequenting most? Go and look, then compare with below.

MINDSET (PERCEPTION) STOPS	
Good choices	**Not so good choices**
Flexible	Stubborn
Respectful	Blaming
Loving	Argumentative
Appreciating	Criticising
Taking action	Complaining

HEALTH AND FITNESS
(PERSONAL POWER) STOPS

Good choices	Not so good choices
Walked to the shops	Drove to the shops
Worked out	Sat on my arse
Real cooked home food	Alcohol and a takeaway
Night in relaxing	Partied till 3am

FINANCIAL/BUSINESS
(PRODUCTIVITY) STOPS

Good choices	Not so good choices
Great book	Facebook
Self-educating	Self-medicating
Solutions	Problems

FAMILY/RELATIONSHIPS/YOU TIME
(PLAY) STOPS

Good choices	Not so good choices
Home for dinner	Unpaid overtime
Met a friend for lunch	Sat doing paperwork
Booked family time	'Daddy has to work'

Now, please don't beat yourself up because you've been making more of the 'no so good' choices. That's precisely why I've not said *BAD* choices.

When you beat yourself up, it's easy to get despondent, angry, frustrated - which tends to lead to self-sabotage, and thinking 'fuck it, why bother?!'

Those negative thoughts and feelings put you on a different train, the "Why Bother Express". And, because you're out of control as a passenger, be warned, you can be driven back to square one very quickly. You don't want to be travelling on that route for very long!

A better way to manage this is to think of your 'not so good' choices as lessons towards knowing more about yourself. What made you choose that option? What might you do differently next time?

Just accept that it's ok that you made some 'not so good' choices at times and move on.

We all make crap choices from time to time. The important thing is to *LEARN* from these choices.

You might have noticed your train has a label - 'I'm worth it'.

Why?

Because when you believe you're worth it, you tend to carry out actions that make sure you keep heading towards progress. You'll naturally want to hop off and make a good choice because you're upbeat and optimistic about where you're heading. By being more focused on progress you'll make the better choices at the inevitable stops in life.

When you *don't* believe you're worth it, you'll try to numb the pain and frustration and jump from poor choice to poor choice at the stops, and rapidly end up as a passenger on the dreaded '*Why Bother Express*'."

That train is operated by a different and very good driver who is an expert at zooming you back to square one while you passively sit there until you get a chance to make another bad choice.

How you treat yourself and the decisions you make at the stops on your journey of life have *everything* to do with where you are now, and where you will *eventually* go.

(And, if you've read this book this far, put up with me for this long, then you *deserve* happiness my friend).

STAYING ON TRACK

Here's another important thing to notice about your progress train.

The train tracks themselves represent something vital to your success - *ACCOUNTABILITY.*

Accountability is what keeps you on the tracks, making that all important progress. You might still idly make decisions along the way, but, without the track, your train ain't going anywhere. It's stuck in a rut.

Accountability is *everything* when it comes to success and getting the life you want.

Now, you can give yourself some accountability and make progress, but, *eventually*, you will have to seek it elsewhere from a coach / mentor, etc., because you're not the expert of everything you seek (...otherwise you'd have done it or got it already).

(I've done this loads over the years and, even writing this book, I got a coach to help me structure and format it, help me with content and actually be on my back saying "Have you done it yet, have you done it yet?" (Thanks Colette, ;-)).

Now, if, you look at the tracks coming from the train towards the word 'progress', their direction is 'up' or 'forward'. And that's because not only is your *focus* on progress, to give you a direction to aim for, but the accountability keeps us moving forward and not dithering at stops for too long.

UPGRADING YOUR TRAIN

Going back to the train analogy, a train needs diesel or electricity to make it run. Our bodies 'run' on something too. That something is health.

The tracks a train runs on don't change much over time, but the trains do.

Modern trains have been greatly improved over their steam-powered ancestors. They have better engines and more capabilities. New trains get to their destinations faster and more efficiently. There's no need for stokers to supply the engine with shovelfuls of coal anymore.

And that's what you want right? Smooth, efficient progress.

Life is already a bleeding struggle, but it doesn't have to be such a hard slog if you make some small, easy changes consistently.

Your train (your body) is a direct representation of your personal standards. We can't beat around the bush here, If you're fat, you did that. If you're unfit, you did that. Your choices created the body you have now (unless of course, genetically, you have some kind of unfortunate disability). With this knowledge, you can be certain that you can create a new body with better choices. I like to think of the body as a vehicle. Which it is, it operates with millions of different cells and pathways, the hundreds of different bones and muscles it contains really do operate like a machine. That machine, or vehicle, if you will, will carry your personal message that you want to carry out to the world. Are you sending a great message with your current body? Or are you ashamed of it? Are you being the role model?

Sticking with the analogy of the vehicle. All vehicles need a driver. And the driver of that vehicle (train/body) is your mindset. The 'message' you want to give out to the world is about who you really are inside as well as the other roles you play. A business owner, parent, carer, entrepreneur, investor, family person, manager, clerk, student or whatever. But, also on that note, the optimistic, caring, sociable, approachable, friendly, wise, empathetic, knowledgeable, integral and confident person who people want to be around. This is quite a responsibility, right? And I imagine you want to have those qualities as you continue along your path in life?

Of course, this responsibility of doing so much and being so many things to so many people takes its toll on the body and mind if you're not looking after it along the way.

There's some really simple (not easy) things that you can do to give your train an upgrade in several areas.

Let's look at those now.

BOOST YOUR HEALTH AND FITNESS

Mental, physical and emotional/spiritual health are all kinda linked together.

As I work within the fitness industry, I've studied nutrition for several years and have found what works and what doesn't. And here's the funny thing for you to remember...

...everything works...

But which lifestyle can you sustain?

Everyone can start a diet or program and feel some results for a while, then the body needs a change because it adapts. It seems to change rapidly within the first six weeks, then things slow down for a point.

Your body regularly needs to be challenged and tested. So, change things up a little. You must bear in mind the real results in life are in the *CONSISTENCY* of things.

Even If you change things a little along the way, staying consistent with good habits is paramount to your progress, not these 'quick fixes' that are short lived.

Remember, that's where most people fail – they want a quick fix with that magic wand and don't understand they need to make consistent effort to see lasting results.

Any new fitness thing you try will cause the body to do something beneficial for about six to eight weeks, then it usually stops working and needs changing.

That's why you see those people who go the gym and do a few stints on the rower, bike and treadmill feel great the first few weeks, then think "I'm not getting anywhere." Your body starts to plateau, because nothing changes; the same things are done, with the same amount of effort. This leads to the same result – slower or no progress.

You've likely tried all the diets and supplements going, but always find yourself reverting to old habits or saying "I need a kick up the arse", etc., when you fall off the tracks.

The foundation of your very being is built on *HEALTH*, because, without it, you're basically, fucked. Sorry, but there's no easy way to say it. It's unfortunate that some people wait until they get things like cancer before they decide it's time to change to a healthier lifestyle.

Do you think your health can just wait and everything and everyone else is a priority over yourself? (And I know you judge yourself if you take too much time for you – yes...?).

When is the time when you think

"I deserve better!?"

Here's how to make "now" that time.

I recommend having a look at yourself in the mirror completely naked. How does it truly make you feel? Ask yourself
in 100% honesty, "how are my energy levels right now?"
What if I asked you to sit on the floor and stand up 10 times
in a row? How would that feel? Simple, but not usually easy.
If it is going to be an absolute brutal effort, your body's telling
you "I'm not very fit, I need to exercise and move more regularly."

It's obvious. Reality doesn't lie. You can't deny reality.

But you love to cover your eyes and pretend it's not there,
don't you? But let me ask you something - how's that denial
served you so far?

How you move and feel will play a huge role in how you think
about yourself and how you act daily.

Consider this. If you're eating crap regularly, often hungover,
stressed to the eyeballs and feeling run down, are you more
likely to make bad stops on your progress train than if you felt
upbeat, powerful, energetic and 'on track'?

Of course you would.

You tend to react based on how you feel and *NOT* what you're committed to.

Are you committed to feeling good about yourself? Or feeling like shit? Remember, you're making the choice.

Are you more likely to self-sabotage or react badly to things when you're feeling down? Yes, you are! Because it's an *easier* choice. You always revert to what you know, because one of the human needs is *CERTAINTY.*

When you approach things which are uncertain to a degree, you face fear.

FEAR stands for two things

- ✿ Fuck Everything And Run
- ✿ Face Everything And Rise

And if you continue to make easy choices, your life will become harder. But, if you make some slightly harder choices from time to time, your life will become easier.

Making bad choices regularly leads to what?

Well, from a physical standpoint, you could get cancer, diabetes, have a heart attack or a stroke. Let's not beat around the bush. You could die young, leaving your family and friends in a mess because of your own doing.

But you're not stupid, you know all this.

If your train is in worsening condition, it's going to be more like a steam train, slowly huffing and puffing along. It won't move powerfully and quickly along the tracks like a modern one anymore.

This means you get frustrated with your poor performance, stop being accountable, slow your progress and quickly get off at a station looking at the timetable for the next 'Why Bother Express'.

Because, when things are going bad, you'll go one of two ways. Fuck it... or Face it.

You know *exactly* what I'm talking about, don't you?

Everyone has had 'fuck it' moments and given up. The trick is picking yourself back up and facing whatever it is.

Your "I'm worth it" train *needs* looking after! Your body and mind need nourishing. Here's a few good ideas to keep you lubricated (ooh er, missus :-p).

EAT WELL

You're not stupid, you know ice cream, chips and pizza are not the greatest choices when it comes to looking after yourself. And you know fruits, vegetable, nuts, fresh meats are good for you, yeah?

So, start eating right, the simple way.

I like to call it #eatlikeafuckingadult because, let's be real here, most adults are eating like bloody children! Chips or a sandwich and crisps for lunch. I mean, how old are you, 12?!

As adults, our bodies go through so much more stress, socially, physically, emotionally, psychologically and that means we're more torn down and deficient in certain vitamins and minerals which you get back from food.

But the problem is many people are *not eating real food*.

Maybe you're not eating at all until you get home late at night, then pile a huge meal into you and massively overeat. Maybe you're eating far too much of the wrong choices out of boredom, or using that excuse of not having time to prepare a proper balanced meal.

Either way you need to balance things out, set regular times for eating and understand that your body needs good nutrition *not* just any old food.

Eat three times a day, like you were taught as a kid. Breakfast, lunch and dinner.

I've laid out a real simple way to structure your eating, based on an idea by Dr. John Berardi, that will help you every day, because, guess what? it's a *lifestyle* change, not a temporary eight-week plan! Structure your breakfast, lunch and dinner daily, eating like shown on the next page...

The correct way to eat (in my personal experience of helping thousands of people) is to structure each meal as follows: a portion of protein the size of the palm of your hand, be it meat, fish, eggs, etc.

This will help with growth and repair of the muscles and keep you satisfied for longer. Then, on top of the protein, a portion of vegetables the size of both of your fists, be it cauliflower, broccoli, spinach, asparagus...

Try and frequently make your veg green, as naturally green foods are what contain the best nutrients for our immune system, and energy.

And, finally, don't forget the 'good' fat. Not all fat is created equal and a thumbful of good fat each meal will help stabilise your blood sugar, reduce cravings and fuel your brain, amongst other things. Never go 'low fat.' Go 'full fat' in small amounts. Examples include olives, coconut oil, nuts, seeds, avocado, etc.

The importance of upgrading your train from a physical point should be clear by now.

The fact is, your food is your medicine, not entertainment, not something to manage stress or boredom.

CHANGE THE INSIDE TO CHANGE THE OUTSIDE

But, before any of these changes can happen, and even before you can fully focus on any kind of progress, you must feel the need to change internally.

Remember, you need a concrete decision to initiate your plan to make progress, and that means upgrading your mindset.

MINDSET

Your mindset is the driver behind the engine on your "I'm worth it" train," because *everything* starts from your mindset. *EVERYTHING.*

By improving your physical health as described above it will automatically help you to feel less 'brain fog' and more open to commit to thinking differently.

HOW TO USE INTENTIONS TO KEEP MOVING FORWARD

You may have noticed in the train diagram there's a small box underneath progress labelled 'weekly intentions x4'.

This is a simple little box that needs your personal input.

Those four little intentions are pivotal towards you feeling like you're unstoppable, my friend. These intentions help you set off your week strongly and resist the temptation of 'not so good' choices when you hit an inevitable stop.

Have a close look at the poor choices that cropped up recently, the 'not so good' stops you made as your train was going along life. Have you spotted that those choices tend to need no willpower whatsoever to achieve, right?

How hard is it to pull the ring-pull on a can of lager? Not very, right?

They're your *MUSTS* a lot of the time

- ✿ you must have an alcoholic drink
- ✿ you must have a cigarette
- ✿ you must have that junk food
- ✿ you must do xyz to feel better

Funny that, how *musts* require no willpower.

The things you know you *SHOULD* be doing require will-power, like reading more, relaxing more, working out more, eating healthily...

This is why these 'not so good' options are so easy to succumb to when your mojo drops – they take no effort at all! Whereas the better choices do initially take some willpower.

The good thing is, after a while, they become more and more natural. And they will eventually turn into your *musts*. And, my friend, you get your *musts. Always!*

This is how you move forward in the long run.

FOCUS IN THE RIGHT DIRECTION

To truly move forward, your focus must be in the right direction. As you can see from the train diagram, the "I'm worth it" train's focus (and direction) is towards progress.

Once your focus is on progress (forget everything else), you can continually move forward.

The speed of your improvement varies depending on the driver of the train (you) being able to keep up the momentum.

I'm not saying it's going to be easy, but it's doable.

TASK: HOW FOCUSED ARE YOU

Let's have a quick exercise to demonstrate the power of focus.

Point a finger at this paragraph to keep your place, then look up and around where you are, for anything *BLUE* in colour for ten seconds now... *GO!*

Now close your eyes and shout out everything you just saw... that was green. Yes, *green.*

Did that green curveball throw you? It was meant to.

The likelihood is, right now, you can list more blue things than green.

Why? Because spotting blue things is where your mind was focused.

Funny that - whatever you seek, you usually find.

It's nice to know how quickly focus can change.

Have a look around for things that *are* green now. You'll begin to see a lot more because your focus has shifted away from the blue.

The lesson here is that, whatever you're focused on, you'll find. If you're too focused on what's going wrong in your life, guess what? You'll find more things that could or maybe *are* going wrong.

Shift that focus to what's going right and think about what intentions you'd like to set this coming week. I'm just about to show you how to set these. Just before I do that, let's have a think about plateauing.

PLATEAUS DO NOT EXIST

I'm sorry to break it to you, but there's no such thing as a plateau in your life. Many like to say they've hit a *plateau* in life when they feel like their stuck. But what they really mean is that they're slowly getting worse. They're not growing, so they can only be shrinking.

The ego doesn't like to be hurt, so we'll blame a *plateau* for our lack of progress. In reality, we've just lost focus.

When you stop focusing on progress, you have nothing set, no tracks in place, so all you do is procrastinate and freeze in fear.

The absolute power of focus can change very quickly, you'll be glad to know. Focus on driving your own train. Just as the ego can crush your progress, it can also fuel it by encouraging you to strive to become the better version of yourself.

Here's how to change your focus and get consistent progress in your life.

THE 4 PS OF PROGRESS

You make progress by setting four types of intention

- ☼ power
- ☼ perspective
- ☼ productivity
- ☼ play

You'll need to set these four intentions *before* the start of each week to make sure your focus is on progress and moving forward.

When I set my intentions each week, I like to break them down into really simple steps. It only takes me five to ten minutes on a Sunday to get my intentions mapped out, so I am ready for the week ahead. There really is no excuse for not doing this.

When you choose your intentions, you need to pick something simple and effective (not necessarily easy, mind you). 'Simple' gets it done - 'complicated' gives you an excuse to procrastinate).

These intentions help keep the train moving forwards, they also act as reminders of your destination at the stops and help you make good choices rather than not so good ones.

POWER

This is your personal power that comes from within yourself. Some people think of this as their "inner warrior" or sometimes '#beastmode' or whatever you choose that represents a strong, fit, energetic and powerful version of you.

Power provides your confidence in your own abilities, your day-to-day energy and enthusiasm. It's also your physical ability to move better, feel stronger and challenge yourself consistently. This is really important, because your confidence and energy are going to be a huge factor in whether or not you're going to move forward and challenge yourself week to week.

Confidence and energy (in my opinion) are best built with good exercise and a good eating routine. It has become a ritual I have followed for many years.

EXAMPLES OF POWER INTENTIONS

Have a go at setting some *power* intentions yourself for the next week. This is something you *intend* to do in the next seven days that will help you progress in *your* personal power (confidence and energy).

Here are some examples help you...

○ 'do some exercise six days this week'
○ 'burn more calories each day – track via 'Fitbit'

Don't worry if you're not 100% sure you've picked the right thing, just pick something that would help you move forwards this coming week for now and see what happens. I'll ask you to do a proper weekly plan soon, and you can refine your ideas then.

Do you see the benefits to this technique? It's a simple intention that, once written down, will give you the extra motivation you need to move you forward and then you likely will achieve it by the end of the week.

It doesn't have to be too fancy or hard. And you can use the same intention over and over as long as it's making you actually *DO IT* and get some progress out of it. If you want to use it until you feel you need a new one, that's fine. As long as you're still progressing and feel it's challenging you, then keep doing it!

A frequent power intention of mine is "get stronger and faster this week." Now, I don't fully know that I will, but I damn sure will try. I track my workouts each week for reps/weight/time, etc., so I know that, to get better, I need to be faster or stronger than last week to be sure I've progressed and hit my intention.

I'll sometimes seek out some accountability from a coach or friend when it comes to workouts.

If you don't hit the intention, remember not to dwell on it. Instead, seek out the lesson in why things didn't go to plan. Maybe you weren't rested enough. Maybe you hadn't eaten enough food. Maybe you were distracted with some overwhelming thoughts in your head. Whatever it is, you need to ask yourself "why have I not hit that intention this week?" and be honest with yourself. (Once I've explained all four Ps, I'll explain more of what happens if you don't hit an intention).

PERSPECTIVE

Perspective is *everything* when it comes to becoming more calm and controlled - and you want to be that, right? Less overthinking, more in control of our choices and more peaceful with your decisions.

Your perspective is either going to cause you immense pain - or absolute pride and pleasure. Controlling your perspective is a bit like being able to "*look on the bright side*". How you see (i.e. make sense of) things makes a dramatic difference to your life. Of course, you have your beliefs, or standards, and sometimes they won't change, but your perspective always can.

Ever been furious with someone then talked it out, got their take on the matter, understood them fully, then thought to yourself "Ah, I understand now from their point of view. It makes it so much easier for us both now."

That is perspective!

And it's so powerful.

So, how do you set your perspective intention for the next seven days? Just like power, You make simple and worthwhile statements to aim for.

EXAMPLES OF PERSPECTIVE INTENTIONS

Have a go at setting some *perspective* intentions for the week.

Here are some examples to help you...

✧ 'read 15 minutes of the mindset book daily'

✧ 'watch a daily TED Talk on YouTube'

✧ 'sit and relax on my own for 10 minutes daily'

✧ 'have a proper conversation with the Mrs about our views'

✧ 'watch daily, Luke John Harrison's 'Daily Boom'

...snuck that last one in there, ha ha. :-)

But you get my point, right?

Your perspective intention is something simple you can do to help you see things clearer, for example, improve your outlook, mindset and calmness. It's sometimes referred to nowadays as 'mindfulness' and, just like training in the gym, it takes time and effort to see results in this area too.

Simply having some time on your own, to be with your thoughts and see what comes your way, is very profound.

You could call this 'meditation', but I prefer 'relaxation' over 'meditation'. It seems easier to do for most people. It's crucial to relax to gain perspective of what's truly important to you.

You may be surprised at what ten minutes of quiet time will do towards figuring out a fresh perspective.

If you want to strengthen your perspective muscle, listen to motivational speakers and coaches every morning upon waking. There are plenty of podcasts, TED talks, and YouTube videos to pick from.

*NB: in the resources section at the back, I have listed a few of my favourites for you to try.

IN 2016, 'PERSPECTIVE' WAS MY WORD OF THE YEAR...

I learned a lot of important things in 2016. I found out I could be perfectly capable on my own as a single guy. I also realised I had the capacity to love again by falling crazy for a lady, (although, ultimately, it didn't work out, which I'll explain later).

Improving my perspective gave me the understanding that everyone has their own shit to deal with, in the way that only they know.

And I'm not alone, I understand things are only as bad as I make out in my head.

Byron Katie teaches...

"Reality is always kinder than our thoughts..."

I've never forgotten that.

PRODUCTIVITY

Productivity relates to your financial abundance, which you *can* progress, yes?

If you're in some sort of business, you're aware that businesses live and die on sales. So, doesn't it make sense to get *better* at selling?

If you've got a job, how about learning a new skill or getting a new qualification to enable you to get that promotion you wanted, and the pay rise to boot?

Your productivity intention looks at what you can do to make yourself more valuable.

If you were to be more financially stable and abundant, do you think it would calm your overthinking a little, leaving you to focus on the simple changes you need to make to improve your situation?

Of course it would. Money lubricates your life.

It helps you do nice things for yourself and others. Remember, you're on the "I'm worth it" train, where you're worth nice things.

It also enables you to genuinely *help* more people, because you're less worried and distracted about the finances and more focused on building strong relationships and genuinely helping people.

Ask yourself, "is this financial position I'm in now, what I want for the rest of my life?" It should spark some emotion. If the answer's 'no', you need to focus on some ways of progressing your income.

So how?

Well, an intention for this side of things could be "network with 'said' business this week" to improve your relationships with people. It could be something like "study leadership book or sales video 20 minutes daily." It could be "study money book 10 pages daily'." It could be "make five sales." It could be "find out more about further opportunities within the company you work for', or even studying "workplace morale building" So, many options, what speaks to you? What do you need to learn the most?

If you know how to make sales already, write the intention to get it done, like "make five sales this week through x, y, z." This is progress, is it not? And, by the way, yes you *can* study money - a great money book is Stuart Wilde's *The Trick To Money Is Having Some*.

It doesn't take a genius to know you need to grow and progress when it comes to financial abundance and your professional life.

And, to do that, you guessed it, you need to set an *INTENTION* for the next seven days.

HOW TO SET A PRODUCTIVITY INTENTION

Have a go at setting some *productivity* intentions for the coming week.

Here are some examples to help you.

☼ 'make three sales this week for online program'

☼ 'study the marketing book, 10 pages each day'

☼ 'write five pages of your book each day'

By the way, all intentions are strengthened when you add numbers to them, otherwise they can be a bit casual and irrelevant. Numbers help with making your intention trackable and more fun to achieve, for example being five pages ahead,

£200 richer, 20 seconds faster, two reps stronger, would feel pretty good, yes?

You get the point, start low, then gradually build those numbers to challenge yourself, :-).

And, finally, your last P.

PLAY

This is a weird one for some folks. But have a think for a moment. How many people simply *don't* plan any play time. It's quite a shock when you stop and reflect on that. You seem to feel 'too busy' and 'don't have time' for rest and relaxation.

Oh man, you need to *make* time to have some shut off time, time to recharge, especially if you want to make progress.

Even a finely tuned, powerful Formula One car has to pull into the pits for a new set of tyres. It's the same for you, my friend.

For your play intention, pick something that's going take you away from the pressures of life and the worries of everything.

This could be something fun, exciting, and stimulating - something that makes you feel truly alive. It could be something peaceful and restful - something that gives you some breathing space and a break from the constant hustle and bustle of modern life. (I consciously slot in time each week to see my best mate for lunch and play some video games - I call it

#BromanceFriday :-) – and it happens because I write a play intention for it).

You may experience some resistance towards planning your play time, especially if you've not done it for a while, but it's *vitally* important for you to progress in all areas of life. It keeps your "I'm worth it" train in top-notch condition.

Some rest and relaxation works wonders. It helps you gain perspective and clarity and relaxes your nervous system. Even something simple like laughing produces the right hormones for your body to remind itself how rewarding enjoying yourself really is.

This intention could involve alone time or time connecting with others, date night, family time, friend gatherings or even just you and your X-box having a night in.

HOW TO SET A PLAY INTENTION

Have a go at setting some *play* intentions for the week.

Here are some examples to help you...

✿ 'One hour alone X-box time Sunday pm'

✿ 'Warwick dinner and games Friday lunch'

✿ 'Tuesday night lads' board game night'

✿ 'Cinema date with lady friend on Thursday'

Play time could be literally anything. Let your mind run riot - especially if you feel life has become nothing more than the daily grind.

What I would say is that this should probably be the easiest intention to set. Remember what you used to enjoy doing, but then 'life' got in the way? Revisit that activity and feel once again the joy that it used to bring you.

As always, keep it simple and write it down!

Keep these intentions handy because you'll be planning the next day very shortly. There's an example to show you how on the next page.

HOW TO SET GOOD INTENTIONS

Let's break this down super simple in case you're stuck.

What's important to you? I imagine it's to feel like you're getting somewhere? Like you're on track, yes?

And you probably know eating some more vegetables this week and getting a few gym sessions, or brisk walks in the fresh air would help you to feel better, yes?

You probably know studying five pages of that book you heard was great would probably do you good.

I imagine you've been following someone on social media who you'd like to work or connect with on a deeper level at some point. Send them a message to interact with them.

Perhaps setting a date night with your partner would probably make you both feel better, yes?

Single? Ask someone who you quite fancy for a coffee. If they say no, just accept it and move onto the next, you're worth it :-).

Make sure you have not committed to achieving "all the things."

Once you have a list of potential activities for all four Ps, you need to choose the ones you are going to make progress towards.

TASK: CHOOSE YOUR INTENTIONS FOR THIS WEEK

Now you know how progress works, it's time to choose your four intentions for the coming week.

Pick your favourite option for each of the Ps and set it to be your intention for the week.

Keep it simple, don't commit to doing too much. Remember, it's easy to use complexity as an excuse.

Remember, willpower is finite. You're going to hit a point where you think "I really can't be bothered today." And the reason you *must* be bothered is that willpower will only go so far. You have to choose long term *commitment* over feeling in the moment to really get shit done.

Think back to a time when you gave up in the past - did you just not feel like it or did something genuinely get in the way?

Sometimes you may slip and *not* achieve an intention. That's ok, *LEARN FROM IT!*

Be aware though that most "reasons" are bullshit and it's these sorts of flimsy "reasons" that keep you miserable.

You're used to being comfortable and having *certainty* in your life. Even procrastinating gives you certainty, because you just do the things you're used to.

But, right now, you do not want to stay miserable, right?

If you *don't* set intentions and have a plan before the week comes, you will tend to fill your time with unhelpful or neutral stuff.

When you don't have a plan, or set intentions, you're more likely to procrastinate, right? We've discovered this. So, let me just remind you of how stupid this can get. This is a story is about Olympic standard time-wasting.

THE THREE SHITS STORY

Years back, when I was a plumber, often boredom used to set in. You've probably noticed how tempting it is to do stupid stuff when you're bored, hence, why many folk create drama, or go back to an ex when they don't want to, or constantly give in to bingeing on food or alcohol.

One day, me and my two pals had finished our plumbing in a bathroom suite in an empty house early, which meant we had a few hours to kill.

We finished our baits (lunches) and we all needed the toilet. It was a very bored me, that piped up with

"Hey lads, I know why don't we all have a shit in the toilet? But not flush after each other and see who can cope with it?" They laughed hysterically, then realised I was serious...

Yup, I have no fucking idea to this day why I thought why the three shits challenge was a good idea, but, still, they actually agreed.

That begged the question... 'Who goes first?' So, we all drew straws and who got the short straw? Yours truly...

So, my mate goes in, does his business and doesn't flush. My other mate goes on top (literally), then comes out practically gagging...

Then I enter to have a shit, on top of a shit, on top of a shit...

There I was, sitting down, wretching, gagging, taking half breaths because of the smell of shit... I finish, then flush, then hurriedly leave to be sick.

Moral of the story? Boredom makes you do stupid things. Make yourself *less* bored by setting intentions.

CONSISTENCY IS YOUR FRIEND

A gentle reminder for you, and I can't re iterate enough how powerful this is, the more consistently you meet your intentions, the better your results.

SIMPLICITY ⊕ CONSISTENCY ▤ SUCCESS

I've done 'Daily Boom' videos now for over three years (as of writing this book) and people know me because of that consistency.

I can help hundreds of people and get new clients because of my consistency in sharing these short videos. I need to do that to grow my business and meet my productivity intentions.

For you, it doesn't have to be daily videos. You choose something simple you can do consistently that *serves* you and others. I promise you, you will reap you benefits in the long run, more than you may be able to see right now.

Three years ago I never dreamed I'd be writing a book, but I credit 80% plus of my success to my daily consistent videos; I know I have ideas worth sharing. You *must* have consistency to be a success.

Think of it as a little bit more effort, but *never* a chore.

Sometimes putting in all the effort can seem a chore when you're not seeing results, but don't worry, it takes time in whatever you're striving for. It will happen for you if you're consistent - like making all those mortgage payments for 25 years to own your own home.

HOW TO KEEP MEETING YOUR INTENTIONS

This may seem a little scary at first, but you'll read a story shortly in the coming pages about my porn addiction and how telling people helped me overcome and achieve more.

No one wants to look like a failure, so, telling others *will help and hold you accountable.* You will not want to lose face and will keep meeting your intentions. Being accountable is key; remember, it's what moves you towards more progress!

Remember to plan the activities you need to meet your intentions in your daily planner sheet (I'll explain more about this on page 132).

Why not see if a friend will join the progress train with you? Explain how it works and ask them to climb aboard! It's so much easier to progress when you're around people on the same journey as you.

If you want, why not join my accountability group on Facebook and post your intentions in there every Sunday. It will be great to let me know how you're doing and see you improve. You can find more details on the website: www.hottostopoverthinking.com

How to Make Your Life Less Miserable

Modern life can really drag you down. Social media is a great place to lie. There are so many liars out there, saying they have a great lifestyle, are grateful and happy, sharing the smiling selfies, the idyllic beach holiday pics, the shiny new cars on the large driveway, the happy couple photos.

And, although some are genuine, clearly many are sharing the 'Facebook' or 'Instagram' version of their life.

The outright *lie*.

They forget to tell you they cried with overwhelm that morning, or that they've struggled with anxiety and overthinking for years. They keep schtum on their credit card debt. They leave out they've cheated several times or that they argued with their partner and had more thoughts about cheating again.

It's all about #beastmode, #hustle #happiness #gratitude.

Avoid the Highlight Reelers

Steer clear of the folks who only ever share the highs, never the lows. I'm all for talking and sharing gratitude, but to share vulnerability, makes you relatable,

It helps people more than flaunting the highlight reel.

When you're constantly bombarded by all those snapshots of perfect lives, it can easily make you feel down and insignificant.

Perhaps you've felt like that, seeing all the (let's call it what it is) gloating?

I got tired of it in the past and unfollowed people who only shared successes.

MY FIGHT AGAINST THE HIGHLIGHT REEL MENTALITY

I decided to start sharing my Daily Boom videos to tell the truth. I confessed I struggled with anxiety. I messed up, cheating on ex-partners, I wasted thousands on adverts for my business. I upset clients. I got a private vasectomy without having any children first.

I like the truth, I know some people are not as open as me, but I like to share things that people can relate to. Like insecurity as a man, being intimidated by people who earn much more money than you, feeling inferior to guys who are stronger and fitter.

There were times I felt incredibly vulnerable and that I was a failure when I compared myself to others.

Thankfully, through writing this book, I can share more with you, the personal stuff I went through on my quest towards managing my thoughts and behaviours.

Because, when you want to change your life and set intentions to progress, and live with more integrity and share your opinions and knowledge with the world, some people will push back.

It's not easy stepping away from being a "highlight reeler". It's not easy showing up as you at first, but the rewards are worth it.

I'd like to tell you a story that nearly made me quit being a fitness coach after all that hard work retraining to escape being a plumber. If you're worried about what might happen when the real you is unleashed, it can't be as bad as this!

THE DAY I MADE FRONT PAGE NEWS

If you Google 'personal trainer inspires terrorists' you'll see the story I'm talking about here – one that went national in the news.

My ex-partner's close family member had recently come back from Tunisia in June 2015, when, if you remember, a gunman had opened fire at a holiday resort killing 38 people.

An absolute tragedy.

And their family member was staying in the hotel next to where the shootings happened and even heard the gun shots. They were amongst the hundreds of holiday makers who were running for their lives, screaming and terrified.

Man, it gives me chills just writing this.

But, after hearing about some of the details, my brain started ticking.

If I had been in a dangerous situation like that, and let's say I absolutely had to run for my life, then maybe jump a fence or leap over a wall to save myself, would I be physically able to do it?

What if I had to help someone else and carry them to safety? Could I do that?

Thankfully, I think I could, because I'm fit and strong (thanks to those power intentions).

But, the scenario got me thinking. With the global obesity crisis and the mobility problems that brings, most people can't move at all. Being honest - they have no chance of running away.

A few more can run if they had to.

But not for very long.

Now, obviously you can't outrun a bullet, but the faster and more able you are to escape a situation if needed, the better your chance of survival.

This was the angle I took for one of my 'Daily Boom' videos (which I still do every day thanks to my productivity intentions).

A rival trainer in my area, alongside a local authority guy who helped out victims of crime, both got a hold of my video on social media.

They said "I was talking about a national tragedy to profit my business."

Now, you know I set a lot of intentions – but this was *not* one of them.

The video went viral and the haters started flooding in.

Clearly, they didn't understand the 'wake-up call' angle of my message, and their perspective was that I was wrong, immoral.

That's their opinion, they are entitled to it. But, because I mentioned the word 'terrorist' in that context, people were losing their damn minds.

It escalated from there.

Hundreds of hate comments were posted, direct threats made, aggressive messages flooded in.

Then, the local paper called me up to get my side of the story and put it online where thousands more could see it.

Then they printed the story on their front page the very next day.

Walking into your local grocery store and seeing your face on the front of the Shields Gazette newspaper, with it's 15,000 circulation, for all the wrong reasons, was pretty daunting.

I nearly quit everything.

Screw being authentic for a laugh – I'm going back to sharing the easy shit! I was intimidated. Felt the world was against me. How on earth was I supposed to recover from this mess?

The story kept running.

Online radio shows contacted me. More national newspapers, the Metro, Daily Express, the Mirror online, and I was terrified.

My friends followed everything and reported back, but I kept distancing myself from it. It was the only way I could think of to deal with it. I didn't want to see the hate.

One thing they kept assuring me of was how much support was coming across.

There were many people agreeing with me. After I had the courage to speak my mind, others felt able to as well.

The support made me able to look at the shitstorm again and I read a few comments.

One was from an ex-soldier who was backing me up, explaining the importance of keeping in shape because you never know when danger could strike.

So, after days of overthinking, several bouts of anxiety, too scared to even leave the house, I read the paper.

They actually stated my side of the argument, except for the ridiculous headline 'Personal trainer tells people to get fit so they can run from terrorists.'

I mean, what the actual fuck? The media will do *ANYTHING* to make a story and grab your attention.

I responded in another video the next day, showing the newspaper article. It took some courage, but, despite all the chaos, something funny happened afterwards. Something positive.

MORE people started following me.

MORE people started messaging me nice things.

> *MORE* people built up a respect for me because I stayed my course and didn't give up.

There's a huge lesson in this story. If you're trying to be an inspiration and stand up for what you believe, you are going to have people that disagree with your beliefs.

If they choose to react negatively or aggressively, it's likely because you're speaking some truth they don't have the balls to. Otherwise, the backlash can happen when you represent something that they are lacking.

REMEMBER, IT'S NOT YOU THE HATERS HATE

Whatever you're worried about showing to others about who you are, I think you can safely say you're unlikely to end up in as much hot water as I did :-).

Be bold. Take off the mask and the highlight reel filter. I *PROMISE* you, it's worth it.

How people react is a mirror reflection of how they feel about themselves and not about you.

You've just got to accept some people don't or won't like you. Take comfort in the thought that, deep down, they actually don't like themselves in some way.

Maybe it is the way you dress? The way you speak? How your hair is? The things you say? The way you carry yourself?

Either way, it's ok.

But, if you're 100% being yourself, many will respect and follow you.

It's other people's business who they are drawn to love or loathe, not yours.

Smile and wish them well.

Let your progress do the talking :-).

AVOID OTHER BAD INFLUENCES

Parents, friends, family, even co-workers and, basically, anyone who is in your circle, *can* be a bad influence and question or criticise your motives if your progress is making them feel inferior.

Most people don't like you succeeding, because it makes them look weak if they themselves are not succeeding.

Remember to focus on driving your progress train with pride, that is your priority.

HOW TO BE HAPPIER

I mentioned earlier that the key to being more happy is to stop lying and be who you really are.

Take the mask off you show others the true you.

Battle scars are attractive and people who see vulnerability, mostly respect it.

When you have the 'happy mask' on, it's easy to succumb to not so good choices.

Maybe you'd planned to go to the cinema and be alcohol free on a Friday night because you're starting to realise alcohol is making you more miserable and you want to be healthier. Instead, you ended up in a bar because your mates roped you into getting pissed and the 'happy mask' side of you went along with it.

Be honest. Be you. Start making more helpful choices to get balance back in your life.

Here are some ways take off the mask and start living more authentically, and feel the freedom it brings.

SHARE YOUR JOURNEY

No one likes a whinger, but people do respect a person who says "Yeah, I've made some mistakes in my life, but I'm trying to better myself."

Be that person, rather than the whinger who rants and talks about all their problems and never any solutions.

You know someone like that, right?

Life is about the ups and downs. I mean, some days suck, some are in between, others are up, manically high even. But, to put it into perspective, there's someone out there who'll be going through the same thing as you, and they want to know they're not alone with their dreams and struggles.

You don't need to talk about the not so good days in a whiny way, but more a straight up way to remind people you're human with human problems.

Remember, people respect real people. Being you inspires people to follow in your footsteps.

You'll not believe how amazing it is to have someone say "I kept going because of you' or 'you inspired me, you saved my life"... *that*, I think, can only happen when you're living authentically. And that means sharing struggles, as well as wins and victories :-).

You can do this – give it a go.

Why not share a personal story on social media about a struggle and how you either overcame it, or plan to overcome it. I bet the response you get will surprise you. If you feel you're quite a quiet person, share this with a close friend or relative and connect on a good level. They may be struggling too.

HAPPINESS IS NOT OBTAINED BY WHAT YOU 'GET'

Happiness is obtained by realising *WHO* you become in the process.

Life is a (train) journey and it's the skills you obtain and the emotions you experience along the way that make it what it is. Not just what you 'get' as a goal / result at the end of a 'phase, if you will.

It's about who you become, not what you get.

The connections you make with yourself and others when you take the mask off are what's more important and will make you more fulfilled.

It's time now to turn your attention to some important questions - like who exactly do you want to be and how do you want to react to things like

- ☼ bad situations
- ☼ people's criticism
- ☼ the influences of those closest

These are big things which are a *BIG DEAL* to a lot of us.

What about when those around you turn their backs or try to attack you on social media? How do you want to handle this stuff? It makes sense to take it in your stride.

To become calmer, more efficient and have the feeling you can overcome anything that stands in your way, you must bear in mind the following point...

ALL TRUE CHANGE COMES FROM WITHIN

The need to change doesn't come from the outside. It comes from within your own mind. Once you accept you're in control, you can take some responsibility for your daily actions and rituals that give you the consistency you need. These are the things you do, that you *must* do, to feel, well, like *you*! They say you truly grow up as an adult when you start to accept responsibility and stop blaming others. I really tend to agree. Do you?

Let's look deep inside you at those "not so good" choices you are prone to making on your journey. Some will probably come as a surprise to you in terms of the impact they are having on your current lifestyle and why you're likely lacking in progress.

Those problems are often the habits you can't you tell anyone about.

You know, either the ones you're ashamed of or are just too awkward to talk about.

Time to lead by example again...

MY ADDICTION PROBLEMS

There are several 'addictions' I've had over the years. I think of addictions as habits or rituals - because it's things you'd do regularly without a huge amount of conscious choice or willpower. They just happen.

I wasn't alcohol or drug dependant in the past, but I damn sure liked to over indulge. I couldn't go one weekend without drugs or alcohol in *LARGE* quantities. I was the party animal in my 20s, the 'alpha male', snorting bags of cocaine with 12+ double vodkas in a weekend.

I'd complain for a couple of days about how shit I felt, yet, the next weekend, I'd take 6+ ecstasy pills because it was so much 'fun.'

I remember one evening going through 11 ecstasy pills, helping my mate build an igloo from my bedroom. (Of course, I was tripping out of my mind! None of that was *ACTUALLY* happening, but it seemed real at the time).

I'm lucky I didn't die consuming that many drugs. I still think to this day that it's affected my memory.

The constant abuse didn't stop there.

I only realised in early 2015 that I was also addicted to porn.

Every day, I'd sit (for sometimes hours) watching porn, masturbating, fantasising. Not only wasting a ton of time and mental energy, but it actually gave me a warped view of women. I did this in a relationship too!

From the age of 18, I was always 'a bit of a hit' with the ladies, and I took advantage of that. This phase was not one of my proudest moments, but life is all a lesson.

I noticed that I just wanted sex frequently, because my perspective was to view women as objects. That point of view led to a string of failed relationships.

Obviously, this was detrimental to those women, but also to me. as I could never relax enough to help myself with my anxieties and overthinking.

Not only did I upset a lot of people, I started to feel a little empty inside after the sexual escapades.

It's difficult to break out of years of habits. I found I frequently struggled to not have porn in my life. (In my view, if there's something you'd struggle to go two to three days without, you're addicted my friend).

Think. If I asked you to give up sugar or coffee now for three weeks, you'd soon see my point.

With working in the male-dominated construction industry for eight years, it was natural to boast about who I'd shagged that weekend. It took me a little while to calm my ego over the whole thing, because, as a 'man's man', we're supposed to be like this, right?

Bullshit!

I knew it was holding me back. I could never settle or gain any sort of connection with many people.

I decided, after admitting this addiction to porn, I'd do a 30-day porn ban to see how my perspective would change, and I actually announced it on Facebook (crazy I know, but I knew that public declaration would keep me more accountable to stick with it).

And I left my porn days behind me on January 30th, 2016.

I haven't sought out any internet porn since.

I've saved a ton of time, achieved more, made more connections with women, had better sex, made better friends and changed my perspective on things.

I now understand people better - men and women.

Sex for men is very much a physical release, a physical need. For women, it's a little more connective than that. But, as a man, once you understand how to connect better with someone, the sex becomes better and you can both enjoy the experience more too :-).

You learn a lot about yourself when trying to beat an addiction. It gives you a massive amount of pride to say "I overcame..."

TREAT YOURSELF TO THE FIVE-STAR PACKAGE

You've no doubt heard of five-star hotels and five-star service and you automatically think it's one of the best right?

So, why not give yourself a five-star package every day?

By this I mean living by a set of five new daily rituals that will help you achieve and notice your progress, calm your overthinking, relax your mind and help your overall mental and physical health.

Before you can check into five-star package land, there are a few things you need to know to help you get the most out of this.

MINIMISE YOUR UNHELPFUL THINKING

When you consider changing your life and incorporating new habits, you always usually stumble into resistance of some kind, which can be many things, like self-doubt, self-sabotage, questions and also statements like "I don't have time" or "I'm not that kind of person".

There's certain thought patterns that you need to recognise before you can start using better daily rituals to go forward in your life, because anyone can give something a go. It's often pretty easy to start something. What's hard is being consistent, and that's where people fail.

Let's look at the two main types of unhelpful thinking that will hinder your progress here, stubbornness and justifying. These will massively slow down or even stop your progress and undermine your ability to act on your weekly intentions, so, let's learn how to deal with them.

DITCH YOUR STUBBORNNESS

If you've ever said to yourself "I am who I am and I'm not changing for anyone" then the likelihood is you're stuck in some area of your life. Otherwise, you probably wouldn't use this statement very often.

This is a very fixed mindset to have. It's going to be a struggle to grow and learn and become better and make your life easier with such stubbornness.

When it comes to being less stubborn and trying a fresh approach, it can be frustrating to try something new and suck at it or maybe not have very much faith in it bringing the results you need.

To combat this, focus on the benefits of discovering new or better ways to do things, rather than rigidly sticking to your old ways.

I know I'm not the expert on everything, just like you're not. However, there is always another way to do something and you need to be a little more open-minded so that you can change your approach to do something more effective.

QUIT JUSTIFYING

"Drink, drugs and womanising is ok. It's not like I'm the only one!"

Think about things you'd say with conviction to re-enforce that it is 'ok' in your situation to do certain things, when really you may be unfulfilled and leading a toxic lifestyle. An example of this is when people justify their pizza and chips because they had a side salad and it makes them feel as if they're doing something of value to themselves. I mean, really?! Is that serving you right now?

Let's cut the bullshit, shall we?

STOP WASTING TIME

You might not think you have much of a routine, but I promise you that you do. And a lack of control over that routine is why your mind is tempted to make poor choices.

Is your routine structured something like this

- wake up: 7:30am – toilet, wash face, brush teeth, kettle on for coffee, turn on the news while making porridge, sort animals/kids' essentials' etc., sit and eat, look at Facebook, check newsfeed, get dressed for work, rush out to car
- 8:30am leave for work
- 9am arrive work and work till 5pm
- 5pm drive home, arrive home 5:30pm

- ☼ make tea, watch TV, sort out kids/dog/housework, etc. relax with a film and a drink, or more social media
- ☼ head off to bed like a zombie round about 10 / 11pm

This is a typical routine for millions of people and every act in this routine you could call a 'ritual'.

This example illustrates that you still have rituals in your routine, no matter how chaotic life might feel at times.

Your daily rituals are your routine and the things that are going to determine your progress in life. They are all those little acts done daily (consistently) that will either contribute to your progress or take you further away from it.

QUIT WATCHING THE NEWS

Watching the news every day is a very common ritual for many. I don't have an aerial in my TV. I use my TV to play video games, watch Netflix and Blu-rays, but the simple (not easy) act of disconnecting your aerial and no longer immersing yourself in live TV or the news will automatically force you to focus on yourself more.

Focusing on you means making better progress and growing as a person (providing you follow up with the rest of the advice in this book).

Why have I singled out 'the news' in particular?

Well, it's quite simple, the news makes people focus on all the negative garbage that's going wrong in the world.

It showcases things you *DON'T NEED* to know. Why? Well what's the benefit to you knowing? How does that information serve you?

To make progress, you need to know yourself and your own mind more than what's going on in the world. Most folk only want to know what's in the news headlines, because everyone else talks about the main stories. People will tend to judge you if you say "I don't watch the news." Somehow, it's seen as being irresponsible, naïve, uncaring, thoughtless or just weird.

But, personally, I like to be a bit weird.

What's more, I like to live with less drama in my life and focus on positive things, like how I'm going to make progress instead of complaining about an issue or discussing about who's just been murdered or what the politicians are saying now. Realistically, me knowing that stuff isn't going to change that situation is it?

People watching the news tend to say things like "I'm so lucky and fortunate I don't live there." That attitude usually leaves you with the feeling of not needing to push forward and grow out your comfort zone because, compared to all the crap going on in the world, you're 'fortunate'.

Yeah, right!

There's another reason why starting your day listening to the news is bad.

The first part of your day is the most influential time for your brain. It sets the tone for the day. Think about the first song you hear on the radio driving to work or on TV, you sing it constantly. Have you ever wondered why? It's because your brainwave cycles are operating at a rate which allows you to retain information and feelings better in the morning.

So, if you're hearing about Johnny Furmay (made up name), who's just had his head chopped off and his family murdered, it ain't exactly a 'progress-friendly' way to start your day, right?

You, of course, may not agree with me here, because you have a different perspective.

All I ask is that that you try it for two weeks and see how you feel. Be sure to send me a Facebook message and tell me I'm full of crap if you like. I'm always open to feedback :-).

Get this negative influence out your life and there's so much more time to focus on *you*, and *not* what's going on around you that you typically have *no* control over.

The five-star package helps you to boost your progress with a variety of daily rituals.

We like to hold onto our daily routine, even if it's not serving us, because it makes us feel a sense of self control. It's a comfort blanket. If you jettisoned your daily routine, you'd immediately feel naked, insecure and vulnerable. You'd feel out of control, and that scares you.

Your rituals are what make you who you are.

Ready to start a new lifestyle with some new, better rituals?

Good. Let's go.

STEP #1. CREATE A GOOD MORNING ROUTINE

Remember, your brain is running 'optimally' in the morning. It's open to things and can be easily influenced, especially when you're tired and overwhelmed.

Your morning routine is pivotal in terms of your overall progress.

How you wake up will decide most of your day.

Are you the type of person who snoozes till the last minute, then goes mental getting dressed, dashes about sorting the errands, shoves a quick bit of toast in your gob and slurps coffee in the car in traffic on the way to work?

Regardless of how it looks, ask yourself "Is my morning routine relaxing and inspiring?"

Probably not.

Here's how to change what happens immediately after you wake up for the better.

Wake up to relax, 30 to 45 minutes *PRIOR* to starting *anything*.

Hitting that snooze for another nine minutes isn't going to make you feel any better. You're still going to be a grouchy bastard when you get up. (I regularly wake up groggy and anxious. Truth. But it's what I do after I wake that calms my anxieties and makes me feel empowered).

A little tip here, if you struggle to not hit the snooze button, put your alarm (this includes your mobile phone) as far away from your head as you can.

Most people leave it on the bedside table. Big mistake, because you're only going to reach over and press the snooze, right?

However, if it's on the other side of the room and it's making a racket, you're forced to get out of the covers.

This could be the best life hack you've heard all year :-).

Once you've hauled your ass outta bed, you continue on your set of daily rituals, right? The stuff you *must* do in order to feel alive.

Here's a little list of my personal daily rituals

☼ out of bed 45 minutes before day starts, alarm off
☼ go to toilet
☼ wash face
☼ make a greens drink (health comes first)
☼ make a butter coffee (blend coffee and butter)
☼ sit on the couch with my cat (Mimi or Suzie) on
   my lap
☼ focus on taking some deep calming breaths
☼ listen to some powerful words as I relax

I put my focus on getting up to *RELAX*. There's the priority. I am not getting up to chaos.

THE POWER LISTEN

You need to be *CHARGED* with power for the day in order to get shit done. You need the you time, the time to focus on calming your insecurities and frustrations and give yourself some clarity time. It's a hugely impactful simple exercise to get up before the chaos of your day begins and actually relax.

Now, during this 15 to 30 minutes or so that you'll have after toilet, coffee, etc., sit with your cuppa and get cat cuddles (if you have one). Hit YouTube up for some inspiring words. You could type in something like Jim Rohn, Les Brown, Zig Ziglar, Tony Robbins, etc., who are amazing, inspiring speakers. *Feed your mind* with the stuff it *needs* to hear. (Heck, you could even listen to The #Dailyboom).

I like to call this the *power listen*. It's these enlightening stories and words which remind you that *you are worth it*. Because the more you start to hear the right things on a morning (not things like who's been murdered in Syria, please stop watching the bloody news), the more your brain starts acting in a manner to serve you, and not sabotage you.

Self-worth comes from hearing and hearing and hearing the right things consistently.

I guess you could call this time 'meditation', because it's very similar. Everyone has their technique, but I find this works really well. For many, 'meditation' is intimidating and, if you're an overthinker like me, sitting with your thoughts all alone can sometimes lead to overthinking your overthinking. Maybe you have felt this way from time to time?

To solve that overactive mind of yours, each morning, simply choose 'relaxation' over 'meditation', it's less pressure. (I find it more inspiring most times :-))

STEP #2. SWEAT / MOVEMENT

Notice little mention of 'exercise' here, because the act of 'movement' is far more powerful. Moving till you produce a sweat is profoundly powerful in a morning to get yourself charged for the day.

Tony Robbins' words, "emotion is in motion" always reminds you that you *need* to move to feel better. When you produce a sweat in your body, your brain encourages itself to *feel* better. And, through *feeling* better, you start to be more congruent with the choices contributing to your progress. You make better food choices. You're more relaxed in your approach to things. You're more tolerable of other human beings, because you've had this release of energy, and possibly aggression, in a positive manner.

Studies show that people who are sedentary suffer from more health problems than people who are active, and I'm not just talking physical problems, but emotional and psychological problems too. There's more anxiety and depression amongst office workers who sit about a lot most days than in any other profession. That says something.

Movement is the antidote to that.

It really is *that* simple, but, of course, not easy.

There's going to be times when you don't feel like moving. Who genuinely gets up at 5am, leaps out of bed and shouts "*Hell Yeah!* Let's go and sweat our tits off!"

No one.

Most of us wake up groggy and would rather roll back over. But the thing is, when you act through *commitment* and not *feeling*, you get so much more from your life.

What are you committed to? Feeling like shit? Or feeling proud of yourself?

Now, you may be saying, "how do I do this?"

My personal weekly schedule for movement is below for ideas, but everyone's different. You could program in, say 15 minutes each day of movement that will create a sweat. Morning is better because, the later in the day you leave it, the more likely you're gonna sack it off for some excuse, whereas, if you do it first thing, it's out the way; the only excuse you have is "I'm ill" or "I slept in."

And how many times can you really use those excuses?

You feel a great sense of achievement at the beginning of your day. And remember, once you've started it positively, these good choices set the tone for the rest of your day. Some things need to be done later in the day; that's cool, just be sure to get it done! The time of day seldom matters as long as it's *done!*

Your daily movement should produce a literal 'sweat', because that's what's going to give you the rush and, actually, it will create those feelgood factors like more energy, more mobility, having more self-worth, happiness, less body fat etc.

It can literally be *anything* movement-related that you want. Because how you *move* is *more* important than what you're actually doing. The more movement, the better.

I recommend things like weightlifting, bootcamps, cross fit, interval training, circuit training, team training, boxing, dancing, Pilates, swimming, hill walking, even the treadmill, cross trainer or rower if you prefer – absolutely *ANYTHING* you desire!

Just be sure to make it varied and make it exciting for yourself. Otherwise you'll get bored and say that "I'll start on Monday" crap again. Seek out a coach or a great group That's going to push you if you can't do it alone or if you tend to give up when it gets hard. Remember accountability and consistency are key.

MY PERSONAL WEEKLY MOVEMENT

Just to give you an idea. Remember, I've been training 15+ years so my schedule may look a little heavier than yours. But you choose whatever suits you best.

☼ Monday 7am cross fit workout – Paul
☼ Tuesday 11am – 12pm strength training – Steve
☼ Wednesday 6am – 7am team training
☼ Thursday 9am – 10am strength training – Steve
☼ Friday 6am – 7am team training
☼ Saturday 7am – 8am sprints / weighted carries
☼ Sunday am – something light (like a brisk walk.)

One final note on this 'movement'.

To keep progressing (after all that's why you're reading this book) track your workouts where you can. In other words, mark down how many times you did something or how fast you did it or how much weight you lifted, in a log book or notebook. Then, when you come back the next week, you have a standard to hit or exceed. You have a benchmark to challenge yourself with.

It's scary for some at first, but you should always be challenging yourself. Without assessing, you're just guessing - and you *WANT* to get better right?

This is a great focus if you're obsessed with numbers on the scale. Get obsessed with performance numbers and I guarantee your results will be faster than they ever have been.

STEP #3. DAILY APPRECIATION

This is one of those things that takes about two to three minutes to do, but the benefit it brings over time is profound.

Quite simply, each day you're going to send three messages to three different people, or groups of people who have, in some way, impacted your life in a positive way. It could be your parents, close friends, co-workers, clients, business partners, absolutely anyone who you like.

Why is this important?

Well, let's see it from a different (cue my favourite word) perspective. You open your Facebook and see that Johnny from two years ago has sent you a voice message. "Seems strange", you ponder, "I haven't heard from Johnny in years!" So your curiosity clicks the message.

"Hey! It's Johnny here. Look, I know It's been a while, mate, but I just wanted to send some appreciation your way for being a cool co-worker all those years ago. I'm turning a page in my life now and I just want to say you're really valued for being such a genuinely nice person. No need to respond. Just letting you know at this time. I appreciate you. All the best to you. Have an amazing day!"

How would that make you feel?

Just let that sink in for a second.

Imagine if you sent out something similar to people you cared for every day. Not expecting anything in return, but, however, if you received that message above, you'd feel obliged to respond to that, yes? And also, don't you think your opinion of Johnny has just risen exponentially? Of course it has, and you never know, one day, you may need Johnny for something, or he may need you. It's a share of love. Those around you need those words.

Words have the ability to destroy or build up.

You choose.

It doesn't need to be a *War and Peace* length message. It can be short and sweet.

A simple text saying "Love you mate, x" to your best pal. An email to your parents saying "appreciate you guys."

I send frequent texts and messages to my best pals. They appreciate it so much and now we have such a close relationship with each other. It's built on trust and appreciation. Think of the great vibes you could send out and how you could make someone's day by literally giving three minutes of your time.

Make this simple appreciation ritual an important daily exercise and share some of your love. Because you've got lots to give my friend. You're smiling right now, I know it :-).

Love makes the world go round. Contribute to that...

STEP #4. DAILY REVIEW

Ever got to the end of a day and thought to yourself, "What a shit day. I've wasted so much time" or "God, get me a drink!"

Well, if you've experienced this, then this little part of the five-star package is going to help with that.

At the end of each day, either before settling down or right before sleep, you reach for a special notebook that is only used for this one simple exercise. In this notebook, you're going to review your day and write down all the good things that happened from the time you got up. Some people call this 'counting your wins' or 'gratitude journalling'.

It literally could be anything as small as

- 'I drank more water today'
- 'I achieved more steps today (via my Fitbit tracker)
- 'I laughed at work today'
- 'Enjoyed time with my daughter today'
- 'I sweated well today'
- 'I beat my push-up score'
- 'Enjoyed a coffee with Ray'

You get the point, right?

Anything at all that you can find from your day that was in some way 'good' qualifies.

"So, what if you have a really bad day, Luke?" you may ask.

Well, I'd like to share a story about how to change that perspective.

EVEN ON A REALLY BAD DAY, THERE IS STILL SOME GOOD

I have a client, a wonderful lady, who shared with me the story of the day her father passed away and what sadness it brought the family.

You might wonder how you prepare for burying a parent, let alone be grateful for something on that day?

She went on to tell me about the funeral and how she spoke at the sermon, telling stories about the times they shared, what a man he was and how he'll be remembered. She then went on to tell me how proud she was that she got up and spoke and was able to give her father a wonderful send off.

She was grateful to have had the opportunity to do her father proud.

I've never forgotten that story. It shows you that, no matter how bad your day is (and I'm not going to say, "you should count yourself lucky" or clichéd stuff like that), I'm just going to remind you there's always something you can extract that was either a good lesson or that you're grateful for.

Les Brown says

> "Don't say 'I'm having a bad day'. Say 'I'm having a character building day'."

If someone can find something good about their own parent's funeral, don't you think you can write at least four to five things about your typical day that were a 'win' of some kind?

Think about this eulogy story when you're struggling.

Not only does this improve your mood at the end of each day, it reminds you whether you're progressing at all. If you're not, that's ok. What can you learn about today and what can you be sure to change tomorrow?

STEP #5. PLAN TOMORROW

You've heard the phrase 'fail to plan, plan to fail', right? (A little tired, I know, but it's very relevant here).

You must plan your day in order to get stuff done. And, although you may do that to a certain extent, you likely don't plan your priorities in.

You may plan your schedule around jobs and errands, like 'go to work', 'head to the bank', 'get shopping in', 'post letter.' Most people prioritise their schedule in this way. Few people schedule their priorities.

Scheduling in the five-star package steps and things that are important for your four weekly intentions that you set will dramatically help stop your overthinking.

If you're focused on progress, your overthinking will minimise because, after relaxing, sweating, appreciating, writing down your wins and planning a great productive next day (which will take 60-90 minutes maximum), your mindset is going to feel pretty unstoppable. Don't say you don't have time. Imagine the difference if you just put yourself first for a little while!

Let me ask you, what's a priority to you?

"Progress," I hope, is the answer you give.

And the five parts of the five-star package will ensure you get that, by planning them into your daily schedule, alongside parts of your weekly set intentions, of course. I've provided an example of my daily schedule to give you an idea on how this all works. This helps me plan what time of the day I will do the activities that ensure I meet my intentions. You can find the daily progress sheets to print off yourself at: www.howtostopoverthinking.com

STAYING FOCUSED

You may be or know someone who struggles to accept a compliment, brushing it away with a statement that takes away the sincerity because, deep down, when self-esteem is low, compliments are hard to accept. But remember your decision from earlier, in regards to you building yourself up, you need to start accepting any compliment you get without brushing it away, a simple thank you will be a great start.

This issue goes deeper when it comes to progress. Let's say, you do something and feel good about yourself, but, when compared to others' progress, it was so minimal, you view it as too insignificant to recognise or talk about. Almost as if it would look pathetic if you shared it or felt proud of it.

Let me say this, progress is progress, no matter how small. How are buildings built? One brick at a time. How are relationships grown? By one small gesture at a time. How are children born and raised and become something? One small share of lessons and love at a time. How do people attain success in any form?

By small amounts of progress over a consistent period of time.

Everyone has a different pace. Just because yours may be slower than others, doesn't mean it's not significant, you're fucking amazing for even going for it. You could have done nothing, but you can now choose to do something! So, here you begin.

In order to realise fully that you ARE progressing, you need to track. Because only then can you be sure you're progressing, It's all well and good thinking "well I kinda, sorta did it. I think?!" Kinda / sorta is NOT progress is it? You either did it, or not. So here's how we're going to *track* our weekly progress.

TASK 1: PRINT OUT THE WEEKLY PROGRESS INTENTIONS SHEET

On the next page is an example of the weekly intentions sheet which just outlines the four P's of progress that you want to focus on - power, perspective, productivity and play. You'll see examples of how to fill out your own sheet in my account-ability group - details in the resources section).

Write down at least one intention that is important to you, that will challenge you to make some kind of progress, for each of the four Ps. You can write more than one, but, if this is your first time, just think of one for each P for now. It's always best to do this before the start of a week (for most people that is a Sunday), but, whenever your week starts, do this the *day before*.

Be sure to print these out each week, or batch print them to make sure there's a fresh one for each day.

There's something incredibly powerful about the physical evidence of you writing things down. You may have heard the expression "the pen is mightier than the sword." I believe that to be damn true.

TASk 2: PRINT OUT DAILY PLAN SHEET

(Remember, the plan sheets are available for download over at www.howtostopoverthinking.com).

There's examples of how to fill out your daily planning sheet in our accountability group, including showing how to schedule your *priorities* in (i.e. the five star package and your weekly intentions, Everything else can be scheduled *after*).

These sheets are a good opportunity to notice how much time you *DO* have, or where you can make adjustments to suit more productive activities, by seeing each day laid out in full view. It's important these are filled out *before* you go to bed, so you know exactly where you're heading the next day.

And guess where that is?

Towards *progress!*

HOW TO CHECK IF YOU'RE DOING OK

Like I said earlier, you must track in order to make sure you know you're progressing. So, what I always tell people is a great start is to aim for around an 80% success on your set intentions. So what if you didn't achieve all of them? For the one's you didn't, ask yourself why you didn't achieve them? Maybe you need more coaching or accountability to get them done? Maybe they're actually not that important to you and you can change them the following week to something you find more valuable.

Whatever it is you're striving for, a better body, more health, money, fulfilment, you mostly know what you need to be doing by now. Make it an intention and *track* it, so, at the end of each week, you've either *done* or haven't done it; then you can physically see and amend accordingly with a tick or a cross next to the set intentions on your sheet.

It needs to be as simple as possible, so an example of a good enough week would be to achieve three out of four intentions; yes, it's 75% but it's still close to 80%. Four intentions hit is awesome, but let's be real, it's real life and, sometimes, things get in the way, be sure to check all your week's intentions at the end of each week to see if you've achieved close to 100%. If not, ask yourself why – and make amends the following week to change that.

CHANGING YOUR PERSPECTIVE

Perspective is *everything* when it comes to progressing in your life.

FOCUS ON OPTIMISM, MINIMISE PESSIMISM

It's easy to be a pessimist, It's gutless. It takes courage to be an optimist, to believe things will work out, even though it seems the world is against you.

I mean, you do have the right to complain - but how's that serving you right now?

Complaining (which we're all guilty of and pretty good at) is easy and takes so little effort. I never forget hearing the powerful words by Gary Vaynerchuk

> "If you're happy and you don't complain, you have won."

I think it's important for you to remember those words and remember life happens *FOR* you, not *TO* you.

You choose your reactions and actions and the quality of your life is down to the quality of your communication, with yourself first and others after.

WHY I'M GLAD I WAS BULLIED

Going back about 15 to 20 years, like many people, I was bullied in school. Constant name calling, occasional shoving and tripping up, spat on once or twice.

I guess quite typical things, but, at the time it was very distressing. No matter the severity (as many other people's were way worse than my own experiences), it sucked. Your pain is your pain and, if it's painful to you, then don't hide it.

To be slightly vulnerable by opening up about experiences (I guess you could call this sharing your truth) is a courageous act and is a beautiful way to set you free from trapped emotions you may be living in, by possibly reliving past traumatic experiences.

The bullying started when I was around 13 or 14, because I started to grow my hair out and listen to alternative music. I even painted my nails black once or twice and was a bit of a renegade. I was 'different' from the other kids.

That caused people to rebel against me. When I think back, I was rebelling against society, so it's no wonder I was met with some resistance.

Spat on, threatened, stuff thrown at me and generally feeling like the world was against me. In school, I was fairly tall, but really thin. And that made me insecure, weak at sport.

I tried all sorts, did a trampolining competition and came second. 'Great!' You may think. Yeah, but it's not that impressive when you realise there were only two people in the competition.

So, yeah, I sucked at every sport, which didn't do my ego much good.

Roll on a couple of years until we were allowed to go into the weights room in PE. I found that I actually enjoyed something, I still sucked, but, even if it meant I'd done it badly first, I'd keep going till I'd get it right.

Because I was bullied, I knew that, if I built my muscles up, I'd get less shit.

Initially, this was the catalyst for starting the whole training lifestyle off. I was in pain from the bullies, so, in my own way, I was fighting back, and, to this day, it still affects me, but now I understand the pain I felt then was to become the strength I feel today.

Don't forget that it's a process and had I *NOT* been bullied, I probably wouldn't have been so bothered to start something challenging like weight training. I'd have probably been more lazy and complacent, but now I focus on growth, in all areas of my life, especially strength and fitness.

And that's down to saying to the bullies...

"Thank you".

How to Stay on the "I'm Worth it" Train

Old habits die hard. Let's be real, how easy is it to self-sabotage? It's a comfort and control thing for most, we understand the process of knocking our efforts and, because it's met with such ease on our part, we actually get accustomed to sabotaging our own efforts and get out of the driver's seat of our vehicle, letting something or someone else take the reins of our life and allow ourselves to slowly slip down in a hole again. You get so far and think "I can't keep this up, why bother"?"

You'll start to realise as you're progressing that, in order to keep up progress, it takes a daily effort. And there's going to be times you won't feel like putting effort in; maybe something happens in your day to throw you off, you get criticism from a family member, you become ill or something else happens. I want to help you in the further paragraphs to stay in the driver's seat.

Throughout your day there will be good things happening, maybe not great things, and maybe there's some bad stuff going on too, but, remember, whatever you focus on, you find. Keep a keen eye out for the small things, an extra smile, a compliment, the fact you said no to a certain food, the fact you enjoyed catching up with so and so. Keep an eye out for recognising those things throughout the day. And, like step #4 said in the five-star package, *write down your wins* at the end of each day. You could even try writing them at any point you're feeling overwhelmed to bring you back up to the "I'm worth it" feeling :-).

People who succeed *expect* problems. It's ok to not be 'ok'. It's part of life, you can't progress without struggle at times. Bear in mind, it's ok if things are going a little tits up. Don't beat yourself up with self-sabotage, you may have a drink, eat some crap, watch some porn, do something stupid, but be *aware* more than anything of your actions. Continually doing these things without being aware only leads to more 'why bother' activities. Think about the solution to the problem at hand. A lot of the time, it boils down to just being completely honest with someone and improving the lines of communication. Especially with yourself. Be honest with you and be aware of making two or more bad stops in succession.

If you feel yourself slipping and succumbing to not so good choices, take a step back and ask yourself 'Is this serving me, right now?' Your honest response should provoke a reaction of some kind. Go with your gut, seek help where necessary and remember your set intentions. Always look in that direction to help get you back on track. Your weekly intentions sheet and your daily plan are your guide.

HOW TO BE HAPPY IF YOU'RE SINGLE

As of writing this book, I've been officially 'single' for well over a year. Being single has got me down at times. But, throughout the years, I've experienced a lot, heartache, anger, resentment and frustration. I've had a several dates and been connected in some way to quite a few women.

I've made a lot of mistakes over my time and have been negative towards other women and past girlfriends.

I understand now that I *chose* to feel that way at the time. Because I allowed my thoughts about a particular person or situation to overrule me.

I experienced 'that' feeling with a girl I met in 2016 in a rather unusual situation. I'd go as far to say as I genuinely fell in love.

The feeling like you'd do anything to be a part of her life. When you see her face, you light up, when you hear her voice you're just fascinated and intrigued. She's the woman you want to spend all night talking to, go on holiday with, spread your feeling all over social media about how wonderful she is and constantly fantasise about what you want to do next to show your love and appreciation for her. She's the woman you'd die for.

Yes, *that* feeling, you may know. I can't fully go into the details out of respect of that person (she might read this book), but I can tell you, after just a few months, she decided it wasn't the right time for her.

It ended abruptly.

I was lost, hurt and heartbroken. Maybe I could have done things differently? Whatever story I attach to this, it's all a lesson.

If you do the right thing at the wrong time., you get pain.

It's ok. Pain is part of the process of life. Without pain, you don't grow, and growth = happiness. Don't allow painful situations to govern your future with potential relationships. It was what it was and I'll cherish every second I managed to spend with her.

During that time, my gut spoke and it showed me that, after all the previous mess ups, I was capable of love.

Don't be prepared to settle for just anything. I firmly believe you get what you stand for in this life, and by living with that integrity you'll attract the right people into your life. You can't hold onto resentment for someone doing what they believed was best for them, that's just stupid. And you'll never be able to accept love into your life if you're holding onto resentment.

Keep your standards high and your tolerance for bullshit low. Respect yourself enough to say "I'm worth it!" And, when the time's right, you know you'll get what you deserve.

That experience reminded me that I'm capable and I'm worth it. And being single ain't so bad with this perception. In fact, it's a pretty powerful place to be.

Please remember this...

Love finds you. Not when you actively seek it out, but when you start sharing it with everyone around you.

COMMIT TO DOING SOMETHING EVERY DAY

Remember the simplicity of succeeding?

SIMPLICITY + CONSISTENCY = SUCCESS

That's incredibly profound when it comes to actually taking action on things. Something every day, as the heading above states, is what's going to get you results.

Not just Monday - Friday. Not just when you 'feel' like it, or you're 'ready'. Something simple and little (maybe not so easy) each day to make a commitment to yourself. What could that be for you? You probably know. If you need a reminder, it's that thing or things you say you 'should' be doing, And, you know, those things are on the left hand side of the train tracks

Remember, you're trying to stay on the "I'm worth it" train. It's hard with society, friends and family pushing against you, maybe not agreeing with your philosophies or intentions, so it's up to you to stick with your intentions daily and make a commitment to doing the work to make it work.

PRIORITISE YOUR INTENTIONS

Put your four P's in the most beneficial order for each week.

As explained before, the four P's of progress are all equally important, but there's likely one or two which are harder to succeed in for you personally.

Choose which ones they are and prioritise those intentions before the others.

If you find you struggle to exercise regularly, schedule in exercise early on in the day first so that you have fewer excuses as the day or week goes on.

If you're struggling in connection with people, make sure to send some appreciation first before you start anything to share that love.

Don't prioritise your schedule, schedule your priorities!

If you find yourself frequently missing out on the same 'P', prioritise that over others. Also, consider that maybe it's the way you're going after that intention that's failing, it's not that it's not important, but just that your method sucks. Think of an alternative to reach the desired outcome and go for it! Seek help where you need it.

REFLECT ON THE CONSEQUENCES

Looking at the follow-on consequences of a less helpful choice before you make it.

You may wake up feeling like crap. Hungover, out of pocket, possibly next to someone you shouldn't be. The likelihood is you'll not be wanting to eat greens today or go and sweat. You'll probably not feel like being super nice around people. You'll be a grouchy bastard, overreacting, eating empty calories because they taste good and not because they serve you. You may upset people or not see those who you'd like to because you don't 'feel' like it.

Can you see how one choice can lead to a whole journey of other choices that just don't serve you? I'm not saying you shouldn't make these choices, because, at times, you will. But, if you're complaining about the results in your life, you must re-evaluate which stops are hindering your progress and plan some intentions to overcome the problems.

Remember to focus on your commitment not on the immediate feeling.

DO THE WORK

Do the writing. Fill out the plans. Be part of the group (www.howtostopoverthinking.com).

Start with the weekly intentions sheet and write something next to each P. Something simple that you could achieve, then write out your daily progress sheet and plan your priorities to get those intentions nailed.

You can't always be fully accountable to yourself.

Even I need a coach/mentor, as does everyone who wants to grow and succeed. Because we're not the experts on every-thing. But not only that, if you think "I'll do it!" how easy is it to let excuses slip in, right? But, if someone's on your back...

It always helps to have someone to hold you accountable.

So join my group at www.howtostopoverthinking.com

Share your intentions with others so you can stay focused and ready for the week ahead.

You *CAN* do this.

You *DESERVE* this.

You *MUST* do this.

I absolutely believe in you, even if you don't fully believe in yourself right now.

And I want to leave you with two things to consider my friend.

It's not what you 'get' that makes you happy, but who you become in the process.

And, one more thing...

If you continually do what you're interested in, you'll do what's easy and convenient. But, if you do what you're committed to, you'll do what it takes to succeed

Luke 'calm motherfucker' Harrison

Peace out.

RESOURCES

RECOMMENDED BOOKS

- The Trick To Money Is Having Some – Stuart Wilde
- Upgrade Your Life – Pat Divilly
- Loving What Is – Byron Katie
- The Big Leap – Gay Hendricks
- Mindset Matters Most – Brian Grasso
- The Way of the Superior Man – David Deida
- The 5 Love Languages – Gary Chapman

DOWNLOAD THE WORKSHEETS

The worksheets you need for your intentions and planning tasks can be found at www.howtostopoverthinking.com.

- weekly intentions sheet
- daily plan sheet

YOUTUBE MINDSET PLAYLIST

- Tony Robbins
- Jim Rohn
- Les Brown
- Zig Ziglar
- Eric Thomas
- ...and, of course, Luke John Harrison's 'Daily Boom' :-)

KEEP IN TOUCH

I know this may feel like I'm bullshitting you here, but I genuinely want to connect with you. No matter where you are, what age, sex, race, ability, I would love to hear from you and personally respond to you - after all I appreciate you hugely for reading this book. Don't ever be afraid to reach out if you're struggling or just want to say 'hey!' You can message me directly at www.howtostopoverthinking.com .

As mentioned before, join my accountability Facebook group and mingle with others on the same journey as you, the details are at www.howtostopoverthinking.com.

WORK WITH ME

If you want to know more about the other programs I offer and working with me on a one-to-one basis, just message me anytime over at luke@howtostopoverthinking.com.

Printed in Great Britain
by Amazon